25 Tips for
Excellent Custo
Service

The Institute of Management (IM) is at the forefront of management development and best management practice. The Institute embraces all levels of management from students to chief executives. It provides a unique portfolio of services for all managers, enabling them to develop skills and achieve management excellence. If you would like to hear more about the benefits of membership, please write to Department P, Institute of Management, Cottingham Road, Corby NN17 1TT. This series is commissioned by the Institute of Management Foundation.

25 Tips for Excellent Customer Service

An Action Plan for Service Success

■

IAN LINTON

the Institute of Management

FOUNDATION

PITMAN
PUBLISHING

PITMAN PUBLISHING
128 Long Acre, London WC2E 9AN

A Division of Pearson Professional Limited

First published in Great Britain 1995

British Library Cataloguing in Publication Data
A CIP catalogue record for this book can be obtained
from the British Library

ISBN 0 273 60974 2

3 5 7 9 10 8 6 4 2

Typeset by Northern Phototypesetting Co. Ltd, Bolton
Printed and bound in Great Britain by
Bell and Bain Ltd, Glasgow

*The Publishers' policy is to use paper manufactured
from sustainable forests.*

Contents

■

Introduction

■

'Every client will recommend us.'

Is this a pipe dream or a process that can be managed? It is a customer service vision that drives companies and it is the starting point for standards of customer service excellence that every company can achieve.

Research from the automotive industry shows that after-sales service can generate ten times the number of customer contacts as the original sale, so it is vital that every contact with the customer is a quality contact. Customer service excellence is, therefore, an attitude that permeates the whole company, and it suggests that every employee at every level is focused on customer needs, whether they deliver customer service or not.

Achieving customer service excellence is a key objective for every manager. It can ensure that every day-to-day decision, every communication, every business process is focused on customers' real needs. While many companies limit their customer service initiatives to direct customer-facing activities, the book shows that there are a wide variety of actions that can be utilised to improve relations with customers – from making it easier for customers to place orders to developing customised products and services designed specifically for a customer.

Without a commitment to continuous customer service excellence, individual customer service activities will only be short-term fixes. Customer-driven companies profit because they take a long-term view of customer relationships.

Note to the reader

■

This book contains 25 practical programmes that can be put into action by managers with varying levels of resources. Beginning with the importance of customer service and customer focus standards, the book shows how managers can implement programmes such as courtesy services, customer clubs and customer satisfaction.

The book provides all the information managers need to put the programmes into action. Each programme is self-contained and there is therefore some repetition of examples in different activities. The activities can be used to improve performance in different aspects of customer service, or they can provide a framework for companies who are new to customer service – helping them to get a broad view of customer service and establish priorities.

1

The importance of customer service

Introduction

Customer service has become one of the most important issues facing businesses in every market. Customer service programmes come under a number of different titles – 'customer service', 'customer satisfaction', 'customer focus', 'customer-oriented'. Their common theme is meeting the customers' requirements and ensuring that all aspects of the business contribute to customer satisfaction. The intention is to build repeat business. If customers are satisfied with the product and the standards of service they receive, they will return to the same company again and again – for major or minor purchases.

Customer care has two aspects:

- **the physical means of delivering customer service;**
- **the attitude of staff.**

A company wishing to improve its standards of customer care could set up a customer care hotline to handle queries or complaints – that would be the physical part of the equation; but if the attitude of staff who manned the hotline was unsympathetic, the customer care benefit could be lost. Anyone who wishes to implement an effective customer care strategy should look for a balance between the two. It is also important to recognise that management and staff at every level affect customer care and loyalty. Programmes that build a customer care attitude must operate at every level. Customer care can operate in a variety of ways:

- **offering customers the products and services that reflect their real needs;**
- **offering greater levels of convenience which make it easier for customers to buy from you;**
- **providing a customer service centre where customers can make enquiries or complain;**
- **improving the overall quality of service so that customers recognise a change in performance.**

The most important aspect of any programme is to focus people's attention on customer care and this can be achieved in a number of ways:

- running **customer focus panels** to identify customer needs and discuss their views on the quality of service;
- issuing **customer focus standards** to ensure consistent standards;
- introducing **customer care programmes** which give a high profile to the whole process of customer care;
- running customer care programmes to ensure that all staff understand the importance of customer care;
- introducing **customer satisfaction ratings** to measure how well staff or departments are performing;
- operating **customer satisfaction incentive schemes** to reward staff who have achieved the highest levels of customer satisfaction;
- integrating **customer care activities** into business and marketing programmes to ensure that the whole business is driven by customer needs.
- using customer care to build customer loyalty.

2

Customer focus standards

It would be very easy to introduce customer care slogans and encourage staff to demonstrate customer care, but the actions would be wasted without an understanding of what customers actually needed. As so many observers have pointed out, 'customer care is more than wearing a smile and saying "have a nice day" '. Customer care is meeting customers' real needs and the hardest part is to identify those needs.

One way is to use a technique known as focus panels where customers and an interviewer meet to discuss their requirements and attitudes to the service that is offered. Using focus panels is a good way to build an understanding of customer needs. That understanding built into customer focus standards which determine how the business is run at departmental level, will help to improve the consistency of performance and demonstrate to customers that the company is responding to their requirements. An increasing number of companies are introducing customer focus standards as part of their agreement to improve levels of customer satisfaction.

3

Customer care programmes

Customer care programmes provide companies with the physical means to improve customer care performance. They are the physical or material aspect of customer care performance described at the beginning of this chapter.

For example, most car manufacturers now offer a courtesy vehicle service to their service customers. Research identified that convenience was the biggest factor in selecting a service outlet. Many motorists felt that they could not do without some form of transport. Service centres which were located near homes, places of work or public transport routes were appealing to customers – and car dealers which could not offer similar levels of convenience were losing business. Some car dealers offered their customers lower-price car rental when their vehicles were in for repair, but this still represented an additional cost and was a poor alternative.

Manufacturers introduced the concept of courtesy vehicles and set up fleets at dealerships around the country. The service was optional and dealers were encouraged to offer the vehicles to customers who were likely to suffer the most inconvenience as a result of their cars being off the road. The programme operating guide identified these as business users, doctors, nurses, mothers with young children and others. The intention was to emphasise that the courtesy vehicle was a discretionary offer and not an automatic offer with every service. The customer was to recognise that the dealership was making a genuine attempt to reduce inconvenience and offer greater standards of customer care.

4

Customer care training

The second part of the customer care equation is attitude – ensuring that staff are committed to the highest standards of customer care. The customer care training industry is now highly developed and there are a wide variety of general-purpose and tailored training programmes available. Videos, such as the Video Arts series on caring for the customer have established an excellent reputation. *The Sunday Times* publishes videos and books on customer care, and there are numerous conferences and training organisations offering individual programmes. The problem is not in obtaining training material, but knowing how to apply it.

Ford have renamed their Technical Training Centre the Ford Care Institute because this reflects the central role that customer care plays at every level in the industry. Technicians who serviced cars were not traditionally regarded as contributors to customer care but, if they did a poor job this reflected on customer satisfaction. Included in the technical training programmes were modules on cleanliness of the vehicle, checking workmanship, using protective covers to prevent grease marks, and tips on returning the vehicle in the condition it arrived, with seats and mirrors in the same position, radio tuned to the correct frequency, ashtrays emptied and most important, the car working properly.

An increasing number of companies recognise the contribution that good administration makes to effective customer relations and they are training their staff in the virtues of accurate invoicing. Accurate invoicing obviously helps the company's own cashflow by reducing the number of errors and speeding up payment, but it also helps to reduce the customers' administration burden of checking and querying invoices. A supplier can provide material and personal support to local outlets to ensure that the same standards are maintained. It can issue material support in the form of standard accounting packages and procedures and it can provide training in the importance and techniques of accurate invoicing.

It's just as important to train the managers and supervisors of staff responsible for customer care so that they are prepared to commit time and resources to training. When British Airways launched their long-term programme to improve the quality of customer service before privatisation, they introduced a comprehensive management training programme before they began training the people who delivered the customer service in the front line. It was essential, they believed, that managers should understand the problems customer service staff faced and provide them with the proper levels of support.

Customer satisfaction ratings

Customer care is a business discipline that can be managed and measured. It ensures that the company can retain customers and guarantee future income and profitability. In terms of customer care performance, the customer satisfaction index is the most efficient method of measuring achievement and improvement. A customer satisfaction index takes the results from a number of satisfaction surveys and allocates a numerical value to key customer satisfaction indicators. A company is then given an overall index of performance which can be compared with competitors and measured on a year-on-year basis. Customer satisfaction ratings are a direct method of assessing customer care performance and they provide a means for motivating companies to improve customer care standards.

This chapter has shown how high standards of customer care are essential to building customer satisfaction and loyalty, and has looked at the different ways in which customer care can be delivered. Customer focus panels, for example, help suppliers identify their customers' expectations, and these expectations can be used to develop customer focus standards which can contribute to consistent standards of customer care throughout the company. There are a number of different customer care programmes and customer care training options. We have also seen that it is important to measure customer satisfaction through customer surveys and customer comments.

6

2

Getting to know your customers

Before you can improve customer service you have to know what your customers want and need. Why do they use your company's services? What benefits do they get from dealing with you? How could you improve your service so that they get even more benefit? Many customer-focused companies commission professional market research consultancies to research customer needs, but the answers to many of the questions can be found in your own files. By building up a picture of your customers' business, you can decide where you need to focus in your customer service efforts.

7

Customer information

Information is readily available in your own customer records that can help you to understand your customers and present them with the highest standards of service. What, for example, do your customers' corporate brochures or annual reports tell you about them? Do you know what their major markets and their main competitors are, or what are their most important products? Are you aware of what new products they have introduced in the last year or what their plans for growth are?

You can get the information from a number of sources.

- Ask your salesforce to *provide a profile of your most important customers*, using the questions in the section above.

- *Maintain a file of press cuttings* on your customers'

activities using their trade publications as a source.

- *Build a file of corporate and product literature* on your customers' competitors and look for press information on their markets.

- *Telephone customers* to ask how satisfied they were with a recent purchase and ask what were the most important factors in selecting the product.

- *Carry out telephone research into future buying requirements* – what would you look for in selecting your next product?

- *Analyse recent competitive purchases of products and services* – what combination of support services and products is the customer buying, and what does this tell you about their requirements?

8

- *Read published surveys of industry buying patterns.* These can provide background information to the independent commissioned research, but the quality of the information depends on the willingness of leading companies to participate.

This information should prompt you to ask, 'How could improvements in our customer service activities help this customer overcome problems or realise new opportunities?'

Understanding your customers' markets

By analysing your customers' performance in the marketplace, you can identify their strengths and weaknesses, and decide how your customer service measures could help them improve their performance. Customer information such as corporate brochures, annual reports and press information will help you to answer such questions as:

- *What are their main markets?*
- *Are their markets shrinking or growing?*
- *What is your customers' position in the marketplace?*

- *Who are your customers' main competitors?*

By demonstrating this understanding and showing how you can help your customers achieve their objectives, you can build strong relationships with them.

How can you help your customers improve their business?

It is equally important to understand your customers' business goals – what is their corporate direction? How do they aim to succeed? What are their key objectives? By showing how your products or services can help them to achieve their business objectives, you demonstrate that you can make an important contribution to their business.

9

Here are a number of problems your customers might face. The right level of customer service and support could help them to succeed:

- *Your customers want to achieve market leadership through innovation.* Your technical skills and resources can help them develop the right level of innovation without investment in their own skills.

- *Your customers want to become value-for-money suppliers and succeed through competitive pricing.* You can help them reduce overall costs by improving design and manufacturing costs or by handling non-core activities cost effectively.

- *Your customers want to increase their capacity so that they can compete effectively with larger competitors.* You can supplement their resources by providing external skills and resources.

- *Your customers want to develop a nationwide network of local branches.* You can provide a basis for their network through your own local resources, cutting down on their investment and giving them a rapid start.

- *Your customers want to build a strong international pres-*

ence. If you have an established international network, your partners can use your local knowledge and contacts to establish their international business;

- *Your customers want to rationalise their operations to concentrate on their core business*. They can utilise your specialist skills to supplement their resources and allow their key staff to focus on strategic business tasks;

- *Your customers want to maintain their market position by strengthening their supply position*. You can provide them with a quality-assured source of supply that provides them with continuity.

Do your customers depend on you?

10

If a customer is dependent on you for supplies, that makes your customer service standards even more important. Use the information in your customer records to assess your position.

- *Could your customer do without your product?*
- *What percentage of the product do you supply?*
- *How does that compare with your competitors' share?*
- *Could improved customer service strengthen your position?*

The more your customers depend on you, the stronger the relationship. These are some possible situations where good customer service could give you a really strong advantage:

- You are the only supplier of a product or component that is vital to your customers.

- Your main competitor has gone out of business and your customer now has only a single source of supply.

- Your customer must develop new products quickly to retain and protect market share and your products are critical to their product development programme.

Identifying opportunities like this requires a detailed understanding of the customer's business and a close working relationship that allows you to focus on their problems and opportunities.

Making the most of your technical strengths

Technical strengths can be an important determining factor in building close working relationships. Access to technical expertise is one of the main reasons companies look for long-term relationships with suppliers. In assessing opportunities, you should analyse how your technical skills can help your customers. They can use your skills in a number of ways.

- *To improve the performance of their own products and services by using your design and development skills.* Through partnership, they may gain privileged access to your technical skills to improve their own competitive performance.

- *Using your technical expertise to enhance the skills of their own technical staff.* By working with your technical staff, they may be able to learn new skills and techniques, and broaden their own experience so that they can make a more effective contribution to their own technical operations.

- *Using your technical resources to handle product development on a sub-contract basis.* This provides your partners with access to specialist resources or additional research and development capacity to improve the performance of their product development programmes.

- *Using your technical expertise to develop new products that they could not achieve themselves.* This provides your customers with new technology and allows them to diversify in line with your specialist skills.

- *Using your skills and experience to overcome technical problems.* If your customers are having recurring problems with performance and reliability, your skills can help them reduce complaints and increase customer satisfaction.

- *Using your design skills to improve through-life costs.* By carrying out value engineering studies on your customers'

11

products, you may be able to reduce overall costs and improve reliability by designing components that are easier to assemble and maintain.

- *Providing your customers with technical support and back-up.* If your customers have to provide their users with a technical support service, you can supplement their resources or handle the support service on their behalf.

By assessing your customers' current performance and future requirements you will be able to identify areas where they might depend on your technical expertise. Your service can be tailored to those technical requirements.

Looking at competitors

It is important that you understand how your competitors deliver customers service. Your customers will make comparisons with your service, so it's essential that you are aware of their standards.

- *Who are your main competitors?*
- *How long have they been dealing with the customer?*
- *How do your products compare with competitive offerings?*
- *What are your competitors' main strengths?*
- *Have you got the skills and resources to overcome the competitive threat?*

Getting face to face with customers

As this chapter has shown, it is important to get to know your customers' business, their markets, their plans, their competitors and their strengths and weaknesses. Only then can you identify what their real needs are and develop a service that wins and keeps business. Although you can find out a lot about your customers just by looking in your sales records, desk research is no substitute for getting out and meeting customers face to face. The sales team are doing that all the time, but it is unlikely that they will be responsible for customer service. You need to meet the customers yourself.

Arrange to visit customers – many customers will appreciate the interest you are showing in them – or invite customers to visit your premises. It provides a good chance for customer-facing staff to meet their opposite numbers and it can help to improve working relationships.

Attend exhibitions, seminars and conferences – you can find out what competitors are up to at the same time. Events like these are a good indicator of what customers believe is important to the success of their business.

When you have made your visit make sure that you develop an action plan to improve standards of service in areas that customers feel are important.

13

3

Take the role of the customer

If you are going to deliver quality customer service, it is important to put yourself in the position of the customer and ask 'How would you feel if you were on the receiving end of your company's actions and policies?' Before we look at a programme for 'reversing the roles', it's worth looking at some familiar examples of customer service and asking what you feel is good or bad about the service you receive.

Familiar examples of customer service

Telephone calls

Do you find it irritating when the phone just rings and rings and there is no response? If the switchboard answers you promptly, but then transfers you to what appears to be an empty room, do you wait or just give up in frustration? How often do you really get through to the person you want first time? Try ringing your own company to see what their telephone response is like – you could be in for a nasty surprise.

Waiting for a letter

How often have you heard the phrase, 'the letter is in the post', or waited for a reply that never seems to come. If you were expecting an estimate or a reply to a complaint, how long would you be prepared to wait for a response? Look closely at the way your organisation handles correspondence. Do you have set times for replying or dealing with requests for information? Try sending a coupon to your own company requesting literature and ask yourself whether you are impressed by the response.

Your experience as a consumer

Most people have a favourite 'horror story' about their experience as a consumer. By looking closely at the way your case was handled, you may be able to identify patterns that relate to your business. Insurance claims, car repairs and treatment in hotels or restaurants loom large in the list of consumer complaints and it is worth asking, 'What went wrong and what could be done about it?'. Was the problem caused by people or processes? What was the response when you made a complaint?

16

The next chapter describes the process of mystery shopping, a technique which can be used to replicate the experience of being a consumer. Although mystery shopping may give you a personal insight into service standards, it would not be practical for all customer-facing staff to take part in such an exercise. However, role reversal in other forms can help your staff focus on customer service standards.

Putting yourself in your customers' shoes

A number of organisations in the service and manufacturing sections have developed a range of customer focus actions that included a programme called 'Put Yourself in their Shoes'. This type of programme uses reports from customer surveys that describe common problems with service.

The report describes the complaint in full and gives the appropriate member of staff guidelines on improving performance. In the motor trade, the programmes are wide-ranging and involve all levels of staff within dealership, including:

- service technicians;

- service receptionists;
- parts managers;
- parts counter staff;
- dealer principal.

Where customer focus is important

A programme like 'Put Yourself in their Shoes' is applicable to any business where staff actions impinge on customer service. It is particularly appropriate for staff who are not directly in touch with customers and who may be overlooked in a customer care training programme. In a manufacturing company this might include: accounts clerks who produce inaccurate invoices, warehouse staff who pick the wrong parts, or departmental managers who refuse to co-operate in allocating resources to customer-facing activities.

17

In a service business, it is the people who deliver the service – the technicians and engineers – who are crucial. In some service businesses, they are dealing directly with customers – engineers on site – but in the car business, for example, they are 'hidden away', never exposed to a customer. Any customer complaints are filtered through a series of receptionists and supervisors, and the customer never gets an opportunity to talk directly with the service technician.

Enlightened dealers who recognise the problem have brought service technicians 'out to the front' to talk to customers or have provided customers with viewing areas where they can watch their cars being serviced. Dealers who expose their service staff in this way and made them accountable report that the exercise has a high motivational benefit.

The same process can be applied to professional services where there is a traditional layer of account management between the customer and the service provider. In advertising, for example, the account director, followed by the account manager and an account executive, with perhaps a client services director as well, all stand between the customer and the creative team who develop the advertisements. The creative process also filters down from a creative group head through a creative director to a writer and art director, so the opportunities for low customer awareness are high.

When the programme is valuable

It is the barriers between the customer and the people who provide the service that make programmes like 'Put Yourself in their Shoes' so important. These are some of the indicators that highlight when a programme is necessary.

- There are high levels of customer complaints about standards of service.
- The complaints can be attributed to poor performance by staff who are not in direct contact with customers, although some of them may be.
- The problems cannot be overcome by quality actions or by change to the physical processes.
- The problems are rooted in poor customer attitudes or a lack of understanding of customer needs.
- There is no mechanism for the key staff to learn about customer needs; the staff are trained in technical skills, but they have no experience of customer care.
- Customer concerns can be identified through surveys and questionnaires, and it is possible to get specific comments from customers.
- Training and other customer actions can be used to improve performance and raise levels of customer satisfaction.

These indicators can be applied to a wide range of businesses and help to identify where the customer focus should be placed.

Aims of the programme

The overall aim is to improve the quality of service as a means of building long-term customer satisfaction. The objectives of an initiative like 'Put Yourself in their Shoes' include:

- *To raise overall levels of customer satisfaction;*
- *To ensure that individual outlets are able to deliver a consistent standard of service;*
- *To raise awareness of the importance of customer care among staff at all levels;*
- *To make staff aware of customer needs;*
- *To ensure that customer focus is built into all training activities and business processes;*
- *To ensure that customer care activities could be measured.*

19

How the programme works

Before you run a programme like this, you need to have customer comments. Ask customers to include verbatim comments when they return feedback forms or complete any other type of research questionnaire. The programme begins with a process of research using customer complaints and customer feedback as a means of identifying the main causes of concern. The complaints should be analysed to identify patterns so that you can assess where the main problems are originating. In the car dealership example described earlier, the problems were segmented into the following areas:

- parts department;
- service department;
- bodyshop;
- pre-delivery inspection department.

The programme also identified that the following people would be involved in the process:

- parts manager;

- parts supervisor;
- parts counter staff;
- service manager;
- service receptionist;
- service supervisor;
- service technician.

The next stage is to make staff aware of the importance of customer focus and to ensure that they are committed to its success. Meetings, brochures, staff magazines, posters on noticeboards and videos can all be used to raise awareness.

You can also use other initiatives to add a competitive element to the programme. For example, staff who reach the required standard in their own activities are invited to join specialist staff guilds and compete against each other to be 'Service Receptionist of the Year' or 'Technician of the Year'. This rivalry can make an important contribution to the long-term success of a programme by paving the way for the introduction of nationwide customer focus standards in the future.

Programmes like this are too important for you just to send a brochure and video to staff and let them get on with it. It is more effective to hold an introductory session and to discuss an implementation plan with different members of staff who have been identified earlier in the programme.

Benefits of the programme

Programmes like this can help to build a commitment to customer care among staff who felt that they have little to do with customers. They can also lay the groundwork for future customer care programmes that are targeted at different groups of staff. By using customer comments directly, they helped staff to look at their work from the customer's point of view and to treat each customer as an individual. The programme also encourage an attitude of competition between different groups of staff and this allows progress to be measured. Comparing the customer care rating of different departments or different dealerships allows you to take action to improve under-performing departments and to reward achievement.

Customers benefit because they receive higher standards of service and they can be confident that their concerns will be recognised. By telling the company about their problems, they are encouraging and receiving a positive response. They can expect that their cars will be taken care of and returned in the best possible condition.

Putting the programme into operation

These are the key stages in putting a programme like this into operation.

- *Identify the people who are the target for the programme.*
- *Use customer research to assess the planned outcome of the programme.*
- *Develop a training programme that will improve staff performance.*
- *Encourage staff to develop their own action programmes.*
- *Measure and reward improvements in performance.*
- *Provide a basis for comparison between different groups of staff.*
- *Get the commitment of managers to support the programme by demonstrating business benefits.*
- *Provide support and resources to implement the programme.*
- *Ensure that customer queries and concerns receive a positive response.*
- *Involve customers in the process of improving standards and keep them informed of progress.*

'Put Yourself in their Shoes' is a programme that helps staff understand customers by directly relaying customer comments to 'backroom staff'. The customer comments represent common

21

problems in customer relations and encourage the staff to recognise their customers' concerns and take action. Action programmes should be put into place to improve performance and there should be a basis for measuring progress and comparative performance. The programme enables customer focus to be introduced throughout an organisation and helps to raise standards of customer service.

4

Go shopping

Introduction

Mystery shopping or shadow shopping, as it is sometimes known, is a valuable technique for checking the quality of service from your own organisation or from competitors. The most important benefit is that you see what service means from the customer's perspective.

Mystery shopping can be used to:

- check that procedures are being followed;
- check that facilities are available and properly organised;
- experience the process of your service delivery from the customers perspective;
- check that staff have the right skills;
- evaluate competitive service offerings.

By adopting the role of the customer, you can simulate the experience of being a customer. To achieve this you must become a customer for a short time and carry out many different customer actions, including:

- making phone enquiries;
- purchasing goods;
- making personal enquiries;
- lodging a complaint;
- ordering products.

When you carry out mystery shopping, you should use a formal checklist to evaluate performance. This checklist would consist of all the factors that you consider are important to customer satisfaction in the delivery of your service. It is however important to remember that you are not a real customer – you have expectations of the service because you work within it and you must adjust your reactions to compensate for this knowledge. For that reason, your checklist should concentrate on matters of fact:

- *Did the staff greet you in a friendly way?*
- *How long did they take to answer the phone?*
- *Did you get straight through to the right person?*
- *Was there a queue?*
- *What advice was given?*
- *Were the staff friendly?*
- *Were the premises tidy?*
- *Was the service fast?*
- *Was the correct advice given?*

Mystery shopping is a way of checking the facts of your service delivery, not of making judgements about it.

Choose the service environment

The first step you need to take is to choose the specific environment you wish to check. This can be:

- a particular office or outlet;
- a process such as a telephone enquiry number;
- a particular division or department.

The only constraint is that the environment you choose must have direct customer contact, otherwise you cannot undertake mystery shopping. A call to a production department that only handled internal calls would not be valid, but a call to the sales department would be customer-facing. If you are checking competitive outlets, make sure that you are familiar with the way they handle customer contact – you could be assessing the wrong process.

For example, suppose you were concentrating on the problem of queuing. You visit a number of smaller stores and selected supermarkets. There would be a problem in assessing queuing time in some of the major supermarkets because they have a policy of bringing in extra staff if more than two people are in any one queue. Comparison with a store that did not have the staff or the policy to reduce queues in this way would not be valid.

Who should be involved in the programme?

Although mystery shopping is an interesting exercise in its own right, it should be used to stimulate improvement. It is therefore important to involve other people in the programme; these are people who will be:

- interested in your research;
- affected by its conduct;
- possibly affected by the results.

These people should work with you to plan and assess your research, as they are the ones who will have to act on the results. Remember, if there is no action, there is no purpose to your research. The team might include sales staff, receptionists, tele-sales staff and counter staff.

Identify the customer-facing process

You need to describe the process which the customer should normally encounter when contacting your organisation. This process should be described, step by step, as it is experienced by the customer. A flow chart is an excellent way of depicting this process and should define exactly what service is delivered.

Product enquiry

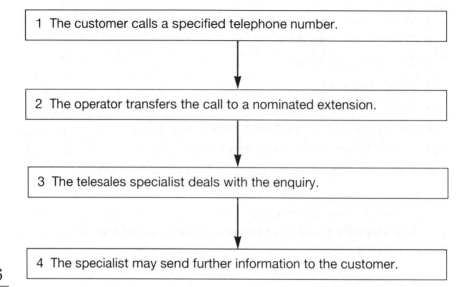

| 1 The customer calls a specified telephone number. |
| 2 The operator transfers the call to a nominated extension. |
| 3 The telesales specialist deals with the enquiry. |
| 4 The specialist may send further information to the customer. |

There are many different assessment points in that process:

- *How quickly was the initial call answered?*
- *Did the call go to the right extension?*
- *How long did the transfer take?*
- *What happens if the extensions are engaged?*
- *How quickly did the customer receive the additional information?*

If the process had not been analysed in full, the mystery shopping exercise might have focused on the wrong activities.

Identify the customer facilities

Now identify the facilities and features that your company provides for customers at each step in the process. Include here the staff actions at each stage. An example from a travel company's catering manual illustrates the process.

- Greet the customer.
- Use the customer's name if appropriate.
- Offer the customer a menu.
- Take the customer's order.
- Deliver the order.
- Check that the customer is satisfied.
- Ask if the customer wants anything else.
- Acknowledge customers as they leave.
- Make sure that tables are ready for the next customers.

Make sure that all of these processes can be observed. The mystery shopper should not be asked to make judgements when identifying the facilities and features of the service.

27

Focus on the important service elements

By this stage you will have defined what service is delivered and how you expect it to be delivered. This includes all of the customer-facing processes and you should have developed a checklist that describes the process. You must now select the elements which you believe are important to satisfy the customer successfully within the specified environment. Any other research carried out into the factors that customers believe are important will be useful here. For example, if customers highlight queue waiting times as a major problem, concentrate on that and don't waste time on assessing performance on the telephone.

Identify variables

You must now define the variables you will need to take into account in order to simulate the customer experience. You should consider such factors as:

- **Timing:** will the customer have different experiences at different times of day, week or month? Are there any peak or off-peak periods? Are there periods when you are over- or under-staffed?

- **Size and location of the outlet:** customers will have different expectations, depending on the type of outlet they visit. In a small local store, they may know the staff and expect a friendly personal service. They may expect queues at busy times because of staff numbers. In a large city store, there is unlikely to be the same level of personal service and customers will expect a prompt, efficient service with minimal queuing.

- **Activity:** consider the different activities which a customer would normally undertake. Your shadow shopper will also need to mirror these.

28

Draw up a shopping plan

You can now draw up a shopping plan which specifies when the shadow shopping will take place and the type of shopper who will undertake the research.

- *How many outlets will be assessed?*
- *How many times will they be assessed?*
- *What form will the mystery shopping take – personal visit, telephone call?*

Check with staff

You should now check with the people directly involved in the service environment to make sure that you have not overlooked anything. It's also worth checking with them that they feel they will benefit from the process. Mystery shopping should not be seen as a threat to their jobs but as a way of ensuring high-quality customer service.

A check with the management team will make sure that you have included all the customer satisfaction elements which they believe are important and which are part of the standard customer handling processes. Remember this research is designed to measure your standard behaviour, not the exception.

Prepare the checklist

Now list the process, features and facilities in a logical order as a checklist for use by the shadow shopper. Each item on the checklist should represent:

- a stage in the process;
- the factors to be observed at each stage.

Provide space for the mystery shopper to check off each characteristic as it is observed. Provide space for the shopper to comment on exactly what happened if the characteristic is not observed.

29

Brief the shoppers

Thoroughly brief the shoppers on what they are supposed to do. Give them an opportunity to become familiar with the checklist and allow them to practice thoroughly. They are supposed to act like normal customers even though they are observing the environment as they shop.

Carrying out mystery shopping

Prepare for the visit

The mystery shopper should prepare for the visit by becoming familiar with the environment they are going to encounter and ensuring that they are comfortable with the task they are to perform.

Visit and observe

Use the checklist and shopping plan to specify when the visit is to take place, so that your shoppers can conduct the research. If shoppers are identified by staff or are unmasked as being mystery shoppers, they should immediately admit that this is true, produce some identification, thank the staff and leave. Each of these incidents should be reported to you immediately, for follow-up.

Identify the problems

Where the observed process or characteristics differ from those specified, the shadow shopper should write a brief description of what happened. This should provide enough detail for staff to understand what has gone wrong and to take remedial action. The shadow shopping exercise is not a pass–fail test, but a test designed to help with improvement.

Debrief quickly

It is important to get the information back to the staff within the environment tested as quickly as possible. Not only does immediate feedback have more impact, but it will enable them to rectify any faults so that customers are better satisfied.

Reporting and action

Report to staff

The first people to see the report card results should be the staff who have been assessed. Many organisations send the results to local branches before carrying out an overall assessment, and publishing results. Any specific concerns or major problems should be highlighted so that action can be taken quickly.

Identify remedies

Ask these staff to identify what remedial action needs to be taken to improve compliance with standards. You and your team will need to assist and guide these staff. Your job is not to test people but to improve service.

Report to management

Report the results of the shadow shopping to the management team, together with any remedies that are recommended. The management team should be able to identify any changes needed to standard procedures and to authorise any action required within the service environment. Make your report sufficiently detailed so that management can see a clear course of action.

The management team should also monitor the improvement actions so that they can monitor progress. Without this, your research has no purpose. Make sure that everyone involved in the research is aware of any change that has been brought about because of it. This will maintain motivation.

31

Mystery shopping your competitors

While mystery shopping programmes concentrate on internal checks, the same process can also be used to check the performance of competitors. By concentrating on the key customer satisfaction indicators, rather than all processes you can assess how well your own performance compares. The technique is exactly the same, whether you are assessing your own or competitors' outlets, but the results and the reporting process have a different purpose which is to alert you to potential weaknesses in your own performance.

5

Who really delivers customer service?

Customer service is everyone's responsibility, but in many organisations it is left to a small group of staff who are in direct contact with customers. By looking closely at the ways in which the actions of different individuals impinge on the customer, it is possible to develop customer service teams. This chapter looks at the importance of building the right customer service team – the group of key staff who will deliver the highest standards of service to the customer.

33

Selecting the team

Customer service should involve everyone in the organisation. In traditional buyer and seller scenarios, the relationship was driven by the salesforce with the occasional involvement of the technical department, but the success of total quality, customer satisfaction programmes and other customer care initiatives has demonstrated how the performance of many other staff impinges on the customer's perception of a company. Customer focus depends on a consistently high standard of customer service over a long period of time and that means building and maintaining a commitment to quality.

Depending on the size of your organisation, a customer focus team might include all of your staff or it may be a project team, representing the departments or functions that impinge directly on the customer. In a large manufacturing organisation, for example, the team might include the following people:

- sales;
- distribution;
- manufacturing;
- design/development;
- marketing;
- communications;

- personnel;
- training;
- purchasing;
- customer service;
- quality;
- administration.

Although this group may not be actively involved in a team, deciding policy, it is essential that they understand the importance of customer focus and their role in delivering the right standard of service. Within that broad group of people who affect the success of customer focus, there are likely to be smaller groups who can help to drive a customer service initiative forward. There are a number of factors which can be used to assess who should be included in the 'main team':

- Their performance directly impinges on customer satisfaction.
- They are responsible for managing change which will influence the direction of customer service.
- They will be working closely with customers.
- They will be providing services which support customers.

The 'main team' will be working to achieve customer focus objectives and will be able to draw on the skills of other 'outer team' members to provide specialist support.

Raising awareness of customer focus

Just raising awareness may not be enough to push customer focus forward. You may have to operate a higher profile campaign and encourage staff. By explaining how customer focus impinges on the success of the business and on their own personal prospects, you can encourage your staff to take specific action.

An engineering company wanted to improve the commitment of staff who maintained day-to-day contact with distributors – an essential element in achieving high levels of customer service. Because of pressure of work and an increasing number of incoming calls, the staff had been forced to take longer to answer calls and deal with enquiries. Improvement was vital, so the company developed a high profile campaign which built team spirit and introduced an element of competition into departmental activities.

The campaign was based on the television programme 'MASH' – in this case an acronym for 'Make Active Service Happen'. Customer response teams were divided into 'platoons' who were given awards for achievement in battle, i.e. answering calls or responding to enquiries within a specified time. There were additional bonus points for exceptional performance – heroic deeds – and deductions for slips or poor performance – the walking wounded. The points were clearly displayed throughout the department and updated on a daily basis so that attention was constantly focused on performance. The results were linked to a long-term incentive programme and there were a number of 'spot prizes' to encourage continued effort.

35

The campaign included an element of fun as well as effort, and gained additional interest through activities and promotional items on a related military theme. For example, to launch the programme, uniformed soldiers raided the department on day one and set up some of the campaign material in front of the staff. An open day featuring combat games and other military themes helped to maintain interest during the event.

Although the 'MASH' theme helped to add an element of fun and interest to the campaign, the purpose of the campaign was serious – to achieve the total involvement and commitment of the staff in an activity that was critical to the successful relationships with distributors.

Developing customer focus in the team

As part of the drive for customer satisfaction, it is important to focus the attention of the entire organisation on the customer so that staff can understand the needs of customers and understand why customer care is so important. Customer focus standards, which reflect the factors that customers have indicated are most important, help an organisation to achieve high levels of customer satisfaction. For a retail outlet, customer focus standards might include the following elements:

- convenience of location;
- opening hours;
- easy access and parking;
- speed of service or reception;
- choice;
- helpful staff;
- product knowledge.

In developing their action plans, retailers know that they must concentrate their efforts on achieving the highest standards in these areas. These standards would form the basis of training and action programmes to improve standards and would be used as the focal point of motivation and incentive programmes. Customer focus standards are described in more detail in Chapter 6.

Another approach to developing customer focus is to 'put yourself in your customers' shoes'. Here, verbatim comments on research results are used to demonstrate customer attitudes to different standards of service. Many surveys and questionnaires incorporate sections which allow customers to explain 'in their own words' how they feel about a product or service and invite them to comment in detail on a specific problem. This approach was described in Chapter 3.

To ensure that you have the right level of customer focus in your organisation:

- *identify the departments and individual staff whose contribution has a direct impact on customer satisfaction;*
- *assess the key elements of customer satisfaction from your customers' point of view;*
- *research current levels of customer satisfaction or ask for comments on your performance in critical areas;*
- *make sure that everyone in the organisation, from managers to staff, is aware of customers' expectations and current perception of their performance;*
- *introduce improvement programmes in potential problem areas.*

Training in customer care

Customer focus standards help staff understand their role in building customer satisfaction. They can also form the basis of customer care training programmes. Customer care training concentrates on building personal skills and understanding of the customer's needs and, in theory, every member of your staff should participate in the programme. However, given the time and resources available, it may be more important to set priorities and introduce customer care training gradually – beginning with the people whose actions directly affect the success of the customer focus programme. Potential trainees would include:

- the customer focus team;
- staff who are in direct contact with customers;
- staff who provide essential support services;
- managers of the staff who deliver customer care.

Training can be delivered in a number of ways:

- using the resources of a specialist customer care training consultancy to deliver tailored training programmes;
- using your own training resources to deliver tailored programmes;

- sending staff to standard external customer care training courses;

- using customer care videos or other training materials to provide a basic training in customer care;

- appointing a customer care specialist with responsibility for developing staff skills;

- issuing printed guides to customer care, explaining the importance of the right attitude and the actions that should be taken to deliver high standards.

Motivation and incentive programmes

38

Encouraging staff to deliver the highest standards of customer service is an integral part of customer focus development, and the team should be involved in planning and operating programmes. Incentive programmes are widely used as a tool to increase short-term sales performance, but they can also be used to motivate staff to improve their overall performance or they can be structured to improve performance in specific activities such as customer care or the acquisition of new skills.

To maintain interest in the programme, it is important to offer different levels of prizes, for example regular monthly prizes for best customer care performance with quarterly awards for best overall performance. The other value of a programme like this is that it can be used to encourage improvement using recognition and incentive programmes. By providing a quantitative basis for comparison, different departments can compete with each other to demonstrate that they offer the highest levels of satisfaction. This competitive element can be used in a number of ways:

- to incentivise departments to improve their own performance on a year-on-year basis;

- to incentivise individuals to improve their own performance;

- to encourage the highest standards of customer satisfaction.

The incentive programmes should be based, not just on current performance, but on improvement and it must continue to recognise improvement over a long period of time. Top-performing departments or individuals in a league receive an award or a prize. A higher status of award can be given to the individuals who achieve the very highest levels of customer satisfaction. A number of programmes operating under the banner of chairman's or president's award recognise excellence in customer satisfaction with a special award for an élite group of branches. Ford's Chairman's Award is an élite pan-European award given to the top dealers in each of 16 territories; they are taken to a top European destination where they are personally recognised by the chairman of Ford of Europe.

Programmes like this help to maintain the impetus of customer care programmes; they ensure that both individuals and departments aim at continually improving standards. Customer focus depends on the performance of staff who are in direct contact with your customers and staff who provide essential customer support services. The members of the team vary from business to business, so it is important to select a team that mirrors your customers' requirements.

Many members of staff may not realise the importance of their contribution to customer satisfaction, so you need to make a positive effort to raise awareness of customer focus and build the commitment of all staff to its success. Developing customer focus standards and operating customer care training programmes help to improve staff performance in areas that are critical to success.

6

Set your own standards for customer service

Introduction

Many companies now claim to be operating a customer care programme of some description, but the problems of running a successful programme are multiplied when the same programme is operated through a number of different outlets. Inconsistent customer care performance can have a negative effect on customer perceptions.

Multiple retailers, for example, know that every time a customer walks into one of their outlets, wherever they are in the country, they should expect to receive the same standards of service. Nationwide consistency is essential when customers are likely to visit multiple outlets – one poor performance can threaten the customer's perception of the entire operation. However, the same principle can be applied to companies with different offices, even when customers are likely to use only one site.

These are some of the scenarios where customer focus standards would be important:

- Customer needs can be defined.
- Consistent standards need to be applied throughout an organisation.
- Customer needs can be converted to a customer standard.

- Customer standards can be measured.
- The company wants to demonstrate commitment to customer care.

Approaches to customer focus standards

Customer care has two aspects:

- **the physical means of delivering customer service;**
- **the attitude of staff.**

The most important aspect of any programme is to focus people on customer care and this can be achieved in a number of ways.

- *Running customer focus panels* to identify customer needs and discuss their views on the quality of service.
- *Issuing customer focus standards* to ensure consistent standards.
- *Introducing customer care programmes* which give a high profile to the whole process of customer care.
- *Running customer care programmes* to ensure that all staff understand the importance of customer care.
- *Introducing customer satisfaction ratings* to measure how well outlets are performing.
- *Operating customer satisfaction incentive schemes* to reward outlets who have achieved the highest levels of customer satisfaction.

Researching customer focus standards

It would be very easy to introduce customer care slogans and encourage staff to demonstrate customer care, but the actions would be wasted without an understanding of what customers actually needed. As so many observers have pointed out, 'customer care is more than wearing a smile and saying "have a nice day" '. Customer care is meeting customers' real needs and the hardest part is to identify those needs.

One way is to use a technique known as focus panels where customers and an interviewer meet to discuss their requirements and attitudes to the service that is offered. A local garage invited a cross-section of their customer base to discuss their requirements. The focus panel included:

- business travellers;
- delivery drivers;
- long-distance lorry drivers;
- domestic drivers;
- elderly drivers;
- handicapped drivers.

43

The aim was to find out what each of these motorists wanted from a petrol service station. The key issues were convenience of opening hours, ease of access, number of pumps, location, payment facilities, customer facilities such as toilets and drinks, and the availability of other products such as snacks, motoring products and, increasingly, the range of other products available in the forecourt. The information provided by the motorists' panel showed the retailer the direction in which he could expand his business and provided a valuable indication of the areas which needed improvement.

The second stage of the focus panel was to develop an action plan to make any improvements which had been identified. By showing that he was prepared to respond to motorists' concerns, the retailer was able to demonstrate high levels of customer care.

As part of a market research survey of retail outlets, a manufacturer found out that customers were having difficulty in obtaining information on the company's product range. When they were able to obtain copies of the catalogue, customers found them difficult to use and, as a result, their overall levels of satisfaction were reduced. The research also indicated that the response to the accessories catalogue varied by location.

The researchers decided to concentrate on two main questions:

- *How easy did customers find it to get information?*
- *What sort of information did they need?*

As a result of this customer research, the company was able to produce publications which reflected customer needs. The key customer focus standards were:

- **clear product information;**
- **simple design and low production costs so that literature was readily available;**
- **clear display of product information in retail outlets.**

44

Setting customer focus standards

As we saw in Chapter 1, using focus panels is a good way to build an understanding of customer needs. Built into customer focus standards which determine how the business is run, that understanding will help to improve the consistency of performance and demonstrate to customers that the company is responding to their requirements.

Many retail outlets are now offering longer opening hours, plus the convenience of out-of-town locations which offer adequate parking, wheelchair access, spacious premises and the same opportunities for longer opening hours and one-stop shopping. These retailing developments, together with future developments in counter automation, training and an increasing range of products and services are at the heart of retailers' drive to become more customer-focused in serving the needs of the local market.

A number of American-style pizza home delivery services are run as franchise operations, and they aim to improve the quality and consistency of their service by introducing customer focus standards. They realise that, in a fiercely competitive market, they have to establish a strong brand identity and that identity is based not just on the quality of the pizza but on the quality of service. Many of the operators offer a guaranteed home delivery time backed by a full refund if they fail to meet the time.

They want to attract customers by offering the convenience of home delivery, but they have suffered in the past from inconsistent delivery performance with the pizzas arriving unacceptably late or arriving cold. The promise to deliver on time or provide a refund is a powerful motivator for the local staff since failure hits directly at their profit levels.

Direct-type insurance companies have introduced high levels of convenience and rapid response into the car insurance market, and shown that a successful and profitable business can be built on customer focus standards. Direct sales operations like this rely on effective handling of incoming calls. The customers are guided through a series of simple questions and the respondent then provides an immediate quotation. If the customer wishes to proceed, the respondent issues immediate cover without any further administration or form filling. Claims are handled in a similar way. The result for the customer is a service that is simple, responsive, convenient and good value for money.

Other companies are concentrating on improving standards in more basic customer-facing functions such as answering telephones or replying to correspondence. Local councils, for example, publish standards for time to answer telephone calls, reply to letters and deal with enquiries. A firm of solicitors has set its own standards for replying to different types of enquiry or processing types of document. These are published and communicated to customers as a set of customer focus standards.

Guidelines for setting customer focus standards

- *Standards should reflect the aspects of your business that customers feel are important;*

45

- *Standards can cover routine activities such as answering the telephone or replying to letters, as well as industry-specific customer requirements;*
- *Standards should be measurable;*
- *Let every member of staff know about the standards;*
- *Encourage staff to exceed the standards, instead of just meeting them.*

Benefits

Customer focus standards help to implement consistent standards of customer service and care throughout an organisation. By isolating the elements that customers feel are most important, a company can concentrate its resources on meeting those requirements. Customer focus standards provide a visible commitment to customers that their needs are important.

To customers, the standards provide an assurance of quality which means that they can expect the highest levels of service whenever they deal with the company.

7

Getting the message across

Getting information into the hands of your customers is an important stage in demonstrating high levels of customer service. If a customer receives the right literature quickly, and receives information that is relevant to his needs, he will be receptive to sales pitches from the outset. This chapter looks at a number of techniques for improving the distribution of information.

Sending the right literature

A civil servant took early retirement and decided to invest a lump sum payment with a financial institution. He called or wrote to six institutions advertising in the personal finance section of a Sunday newspaper.

The three companies that he telephoned responded in different ways:

- One asked for his address.
- One took his address and asked how much he wanted to invest.
- One asked about his plans and current situation and suggested a meeting with a consultant.

When the literature arrived, it reflected the pattern of the telephone response.

- The first 'parcel' contained every piece of literature produced by the institution.

- The second contained a selection of investment brochures aimed at his own income bracket.
- The third provided an overview of the relevant options available, a reply card to request specific items of literature and a freephone number to arrange an appointment with a consultant.

The postal responses followed a similar pattern:

- The first two institutions mailed general literature 'parcels'.
- The third responded to the initial coupon by telephoning the investor and asking about his requirements before sending a tailored literature package.

48 Mechanical process or customer relationship

When the investor had received all the literature, he was faced with a difficult choice. Should he choose the institutions which had the resources to send him a large sumptuous literature pack or should he deal with an institution that was interested in his specific needs? His preference was for the tailored approach. He wanted to deal with an institution that did not simply respond to a request for literature, but treated him as an individual from the outset.

Making the most of literature requests

How can you ensure that this approach works?

- *Provide prospects with a simple response mechanism, such as freepost or freephone.*
- *With postal responses, include a mechanism for capturing essential data.*
- *Follow up postal requests with a phone call to obtain a more detailed profile of the customer's needs.*
- *Only send literature that is relevant to the customer.*
- *Offer the customer a contact point for further advice and*

information.

- *Try to arrange a sales appointment to move the prospect further along the decision-making process.*

Literature can be used as the starting point for developing a relationship with the customer. By taking the trouble to find out more about the customer's needs, you can demonstrate high levels of customer care from the outset.

Three steps to speeding up literature distribution

Do your customers always ask for up-to-date technical or product information in a hurry? You could spend a fortune setting up distribution channels or using express post. Fax could be the answer. Here are three essential stages:

1 *Design your product information to fit a format that can be easily faxed* – single sheet, minimal illustrations, plenty of sub-headings to guide the reader, and a clear typeface that will still be legible even after faxing.

2 *Use your own fax to circulate information to your customers or use a fax bureau for large-scale distribution.*

3 *Consider setting up a 'fax on demand' programme.* Customers respond to a series of telephone messages originated by a computer and use their telephone keypad to enter codes for the appropriate literature and their own fax number. The information is sent back automatically to the caller's fax number.

Literature at exhibitions

Many companies are now looking closely at the way they distribute literature at exhibitions. Although exhibitions are an ideal place to meet customers, the people who collect literature may

49

not be the most important prospects. There is a risk that your important customers could receive a second-rate service. Chances are the collector is a junior member of staff, sent to the exhibition to keep up-to-date. The brochures provide evidence of attendance, but do they actually influence the decision to buy? Does a diminishing pile of brochures necessarily mean that the exhibition has been a success?

An increasing number of companies are questioning the free availability of literature on the stand and instead using tele-marketing to weed out the true and worthwhile decision-makers. Here's how it works.

- Visitors fill in a literature request coupon, giving company, personal or education course details and responsibility.

- After the exhibition, a telemarketing team contact visitors individually to confirm their interest and request further information.

- Each lead is then tracked and followed up by the sales team. Results are monitored against future sales.

Given the cost of publications, this can reduce waste considerably and ensure that genuine prospects are handled professionally. It also demonstrates customer service by ensuring that genuine prospects receive a quality service.

Making it easy to obtain information

Recent research from the telecommunications industry suggests that around 76 per cent of calls are not completed at the first attempt. The extension is engaged, the contact is not there, or the caller got through to the wrong extension. Of those calls 50 per cent were single-directional – the callers did not want to have a discussion, they just wanted to place an order or leave information. This can be frustrating for anyone who wants to obtain literature or get further information, so how can you make it easier for customers to make contact?

One solution would be to appoint more people to answer the phone, but that could be expensive and may not be cost effective. Is the solution to set up a central message centre? The research does little to encourage this approach. Of telephone messages taken by a third party 90 per cent are believed to be inaccurate or incomplete in some way.

Voicemail is another possible solution. At its simplest, voice-mail is the electronic equivalent of a personal mailbox. Callers can leave messages knowing that their contact will deal with them on their return. There is no problem in the accuracy of message handling and messages can be communicated to other people in the organisation.

Voicemail can also be used as the basis of a sophisticated customer response system. For example, by keying certain digits, the caller can access information services, request literature, leave a private message, get through to an operator or initiate other actions.

51

By providing these options, a company can develop a customer-focused response mechanism that demonstrates high levels of customer care and convenience. Among the possible options are:

- **24-hour ordering systems that do not require staff presence;**
- **literature request service;**
- **dial-up price or delivery information service.**

Voicemail can be seen as an impersonal, machine-based system, but the customer service benefits are considerable.

8

Improving customer service skills

This chapter provides an introduction to a series of practical management exercises which delegates can put into immediate operation in their own organisation. The suggested sessions would provide junior and middle managers with suggested programmes and activities which are within their experience and responsibility and this allows a 'hands-on' approach to customer service training.

The activities cover the most important aspects of customer service management. They can therefore be used as the basis of a structured, comprehensive customer service course, or used selectively to improve performance or update managers on specific aspects of customer service.

Aims of a management training programme

The programme would help managers to develop supervisory skills so that they can identify priorities and help their staff develop their service performance. It would concentrate on improving the management of customer service, rather than the development of personal skills – the development of personal skills is outside the scope of a book like this and requires a higher degree of personal instruction and interaction. The programme will enable managers to participate in the development of customer service activities which can be put into immediate operation in their own organisations. It will help managers identify priority areas in their customer service activities.

For convenience, the activities are grouped into 13 areas:

- building a team;
- focusing on the customer;
- customer service standards;
- incident management;
- customer contact;
- handling complaints;
- customer relationships;
- the service contribution;
- adding value;
- making it easy to buy;
- freeing people for customer service;
- measuring customer service performance;
- management summary.

Training methods

The exercises described in this chapter can be used to support a number of training techniques, including:

- group discussion sessions to build understanding and awareness of customer service issues;
- practical group and small team exercises and presentations to enable delegates to develop customer service initiatives;
- reviews of current practice, showing how other organisations manage and implement customer service activities;
- problem solving activities;
- brainstorming sessions to improve specific customer service activities;
- role-play sessions.

The exercises

These are only outlines of suggested training exercises. A manager or training specialist would need to develop each of the activities further and prepare examples specific to an organisation.

BUILDING A TEAM

Rate their contribution

A group exercise in which managers discuss which departments, groups and individuals in the organisation contribute to customer service, directly or indirectly. Managers are asked to rate the contributions of the people they have identified. The session will help managers understand the contributions different people make, and help them to focus on management priorities.

55

It's not my problem

Role-play exercise based on a case history of a customer service 'disaster'. Managers take on the role of departmental managers and attempt to 'pass the buck'. The session will help managers understand the process of 'owning a problem' and developing a team approach to problem-solving in customer service.

Supporting the troops

A series of small team exercises in which managers prepare a proposal showing how their department could provide better support to the 'front line troops' – the staff who are in face-to-face contact with customers.

The session will help managers understand that customer service cannot simply be left to the specialists; each department must contribute to overall customer service performance.

What's my line?

A variation of the radio/TV panel game, in which teams of managers compete against each other to develop the best job specification and skills profile for a group of customer service staff. Managers will gain a better insight into the process of selecting and managing customer service staff.

Customer service audit

A session for senior and middle managers to help them assess the level of understanding and awareness of customer service within their organisation. The session will provide step-by-step guidelines to planning, operating and assessing the results of an audit.

For internal consumption only

A group discussion to demonstrate that customer service begins at home. Individual managers are asked to identify the departments who are their immediate 'customers' and make proposals for improving the service to those departments. The group then discusses the impact those improvements might have on the overall quality of service to external customers. This session is designed to improve understanding of customer needs and to build team spirit.

FOCUSING ON THE CUSTOMER

Horror stories

An introductory session to help managers understand the role of service from the customer's point of view. Managers take it in turn to describe horror stories about everyday experiences such as travelling, shopping, banks, insurance, holidays, car repairs, medical treatment. The group is asked to identify the key customer concerns in each situation and to recommend how customer service could be used to improve the customer's experience. The session will help managers translate their personal experience as customers into a customer-focused attitude.

Put yourself in their shoes

Another session to help managers understand the role of service from the customer's point of view. Managers are asked to review a series of customer complaints taken from different types of customer satisfaction survey. Groups of managers are asked to identify who in the organisation is ultimately responsible for causing the problem. The group is also asked how they would make the appropriate department or individual aware of the customer's needs. The session will help managers raise awareness of customer needs amongst groups who are not in direct contact with customers.

57

Running a customer focus group

A session for customer service managers to help them run customer focus groups. The session will provide step-by-step guidelines to planning, operating and assessing the results of a customer focus group.

Getting to know you

A session to help managers find out more about their customers' needs.
Managers will be given an example of a survey into customer needs and asked to develop their own questionnaire. The session will help managers to decide what they need to know about their customers' needs and gather relevant information as a basis for improving customer service.

Day-to-day data

Research can be valuable in finding out what customers need, but raw data can be meaningless to the people who need it most – the staff who deliver customer service. This session will help managers interpret research data and turn it into 'flesh and blood' communications that clearly explain to staff at all levels what customers want.

CUSTOMER SERVICE STANDARDS

Never mind the quality

This session will help managers understand why quality is so important to customer service. It will provide managers with examples of current practice and ask them to identify activities in their own organisation where quality processes could be used to improve customer service.

58

Personal service

This session is designed to help managers raise customer service standards by personal example. It asks managers to identify personal tasks or skills that impinge on customer service and prepare a personal action plan for applying quality processes to themselves. This session will enable managers to improve team performance through effective leadership.

Setting the standards

Every organisation should have customer focus standards which provide guidelines on how staff should deal with customers to achieve the highest levels of customer satisfaction. This session will give managers a step-by-step guide to identifying the key customer focus activities within their organisation and estab-lishing a set of standards that are relevant, practicable and measurable.

Local heroes

A session for companies who market their products through

local outlets. The session is designed to help managers understand how differences in local market conditions should be reflected in their customer focus standards. Managers will be asked to assess their basic customer focus standards against a series of local market profiles and suggest appropriate modifications. The session will enable managers to prepare customised standards that provide the right level of service to each local market.

Arm's length

A session for companies who market their products through distributors, agents or third-party vendors. The session explains the problems of building customer care through staff who are not part of the organisation and provides examples of successful distributor customer care programmes. Managers use the examples to plan a programme for their own distributor network.

59

INCIDENT MANAGEMENT

Disaster!

An exercise to improve managers' performance in dealing with customer-service problems. A fictitious incident is used as the basis and managers are asked to prepare an action plan which deals with the immediate problem, demonstrates high levels of customer care and incorporates procedures to prevent the disaster recurring. This session will help managers prepare for customer service problems and encourage them to take preventative action.

Escalation

Not all customer service problems can be solved by the people on the front line; they may not have the resources or the authority to take appropriate action. This session will help managers identify when a problem needs to be brought to the attention of senior managers and describes the escalation procedures for a number of different business scenarios. The session will help managers to plan and implement escalation procedures for their own organisation.

A measure of reassurance

Research shows that customers who have a problem are content to wait a reasonable time for a solution, provided they are reassured that help is on the way. This session helps managers to develop a customer contact strategy which can be used to keep customers informed during an incident. Using a case history, managers are asked to identify the key contact points during the incident and apply measures so that the process can be monitored and managed. The session will help managers to improve the quality of their response to customer problems.

CUSTOMER CONTACT

Every contact counts

Research in the automotive industry shows that manufacturers make about 1 million contacts per year for car sales, but more than 5 million contacts for aftersales activities. This session will help managers understand why every contact between customer and supplier must be a quality contact. Managers are asked to identify all the potential contact points in their organisation and develop a method of assessing the quality or weakness of those contacts. This exercise will help managers plan their own customer contact strategy.

Decent exposure

This session will help companies develop a positive customer contact strategy. Managers review current communications, including advertisements, brochures, press releases and other promotional material to see whether customer care messages are communicated effectively. Examples of effective customer care communications are included to demonstrate best practice and managers are asked to consider improvements to their own material. The session will help managers understand and contribute to the communications process.

I just called to say ...

This session looks at opportunities to improve customer contact through the telephone. It provides managers with a review of current practice and asks them to identify opportunities in their own sales and aftersales process where telephone contact will improve the quality of customer care. The session will complement telephone skills training courses by showing how managers can put those skills into action.

'Response-ability'

How quickly should a company respond to customer enquiries? In this role-playing exercise, selected managers take on the role of a customer service correspondent and are given customer queries to deal with. They are asked to list the information they need to provide the customer with an effective response and to give an indication of the time it would take to obtain the information. This session will introduce the concept of response times and help managers to focus on the information systems needed to support customer service staff.

HANDLING COMPLAINTS

Where are they now?

A session to introduce the concept of complaints handling. Man-

61

agers are asked to recall important customers who have moved to competitors within a specific time frame, for example the last one, two or five years. They are asked if the customer gave a reason for changing or if they could identify the problems which led to the change. The group then discusses whether the customer's problem could have been resolved and the business saved. The session will help managers to recognise that complaints represent both a problem and an opportunity to respond positively and improve customer relations.

Talking with their feet

A customer who has a problem, but does not complain, represents a lost opportunity. By positively encouraging customers to complain, a company can prevent them 'talking with their feet'. This session provides examples of a number of different complaints mechanisms and gives practical guidelines on setting them up. Managers are asked to prepare a proposal for implementing or improving the complaints mechanism in their organisation.

Problem or opportunity?

This session helps managers to turn complaints into improvements in customer service. By analysing complaints and initiating improvement programmes based on the complaints, an organisation can deliver a service that is focused on customer needs. Managers are given examples of complaints from fictitious organisations and asked to set up a review mechanism which involves appropriate departments. This session will help managers develop a positive approach to complaints management within their organisation.

CUSTOMER RELATIONSHIPS

Meaningful relationships

Partnership provides opportunities to improve long-term relationships between customer and supplier. This session will provide managers with examples of partnership in action and ask them to identify the key factors behind the partnership. Managers are then asked to identify potential partners from their own customer base and explain how the partnership would benefit both customer and supplier. The session will help managers to understand the potential of partnership for their organisation.

Ripping up the organisation chart

63

Conventional organisation charts put the emphasis on a hierarchical structure. However, in an organisation committed to customer service, this is no longer appropriate. This session asks managers to look at their own organisation from the point of view of the customer and to create a structure which puts customer-facing staff at the top, with everyone else in the organisation supporting their efforts. The session will help managers understand how they can make best use of their resources to deliver the highest standards of customer service.

Farmers and hunters

This session will help managers understand the contribution of the salesforce to improved customer service. The session will explain how the salesforce role changes from 'hunters', who meet short-term sales targets, to 'farmers', who build long-term relationships with customers. Managers will be asked to assess the role of their salesforce and to identify areas where the salesforce need internal support to improve their performance as 'farmers'. The session will help managers to build a support organisation to optimise customer service.

Your place or ours?

Partnership and joint ventures can improve customer relationships by enabling companies to benefit from each others' skills and resources. This session shows managers how to identify opportunities for working together, for example, on research projects, technical development programmes or joint marketing initiatives. Managers are asked to suggest suitable projects for joint ventures with their customers and to identify the key people on both sides who would be involved in the project. The session will help managers gain a better understanding of the nature and benefits of partnership.

ADDING VALUE

How do they score?

This session introduces managers to the concept of added value by reviewing a number of competitive products. Managers will be asked to assess each of the products – car or household insurance policies, for example – to see which offers the highest added value and highest levels of customer service. The session will help managers understand the relationship between added value and customer service.

One plus one equals three

In this practical exercise, managers are asked to take a number of their company's products and improve their customer appeal by adding new features or services. The group reviews the new products against competitive offerings to see whether the product should be further refined. This session will help managers understand the practical process of adding value.

At your convenience

A session to show how improving convenience can add value to a product or service. Using examples of programmes such as courtesy cars, longer opening hours, telephone banking and electronic payment, managers are asked to assess their company's service to customers and to discuss how levels of convenience could be improved. The session will help managers to understand the relationship between convenience and customer service, and will enable them to improve levels of convenience.

THE SERVICE CONTRIBUTION

After the sale is over

65

The aftermarket provides the greatest opportunity to improve customer service. This session will help managers understand the scope of aftersales service. Managers will be asked to discuss a range of consumer durables such as cars, washing machines and home computers, and to decide what types of service they felt would be most useful. The session introduces the concept of aftercare and helps managers understand aftercare from the point of view of the customer.

Life cycles

The way in which customers use products can provide clues to the levels of service they need. This session introduces managers to the concept of the life cycle and shows how customers' needs change at different stages of the life cycle. For example, when a company buys a new computer system, it goes through start-up, early life, maturity and growth stages; services such as training, project management, advice and guidance and maintenance can help the customer overcome any short-term problems at each stage. In this session, managers are asked to work out the life cycle stages for a number of different products and select the most relevant services at each stage. The session helps managers understand the concept of the life cycle and the contribution of services.

A piece of your mind

This session explains the importance of advice and guidance in improving levels of customer service. Increasingly, companies are realising that they can use the skills and experience of their staff to help their customers improve the performance of their own business. Managers are asked to identify skills and services within their own organisation which could be offered to customers in the form of consultancy or contract services. The session will help managers use the skills and resources available within their organisation to improve levels of customer service.

66

Supporting the core business

Increasingly, companies are using outside sources to provide non-essential services such as maintenenance and distribution so that they can concentrate on their 'core business'. This provides a valuable opportunity for companies to build closer relationships with their customers by supporting them with quality services. In this session managers will be asked to analyse a number of different companies, identify their core business and suggest the types of service that would help the companies improve their business performance. The session will help managers understand the nature of core business development and use it to improve levels of customer service.

MAKING IT EASY TO BUY

What's on the menu?

Shock at the size of the final bill for service or repairs is a common customer complaint. This session introduces managers to the concept of 'menu pricing' as a means of making it easier to buy, and improving customer satisfaction. Managers review examples of menu pricing from different markets and prepare proposals for menus for their own products or services. The session will help managers enhance customer service by improving the presentation of pricing.

Has it got all the knobs?

Providing customers with clear product information can make it easier for customers to buy and improve customer satisfaction. This session looks at ways of improving the presentation of product information and making it relevant to the needs of different types of customer. Managers are given technical descriptions of various products and asked to list the key benefits for different buyers, including experts, non-specialists, professional buyers, consumers. The session will help managers understand the information needs of different types of customer and improve customer service at the point-of-sale.

Customer reception

The customer's first point of contact with an organisation is via the telephone or at a reception point. This session shows how public and commercial organisations have tackled customer reception in different ways, using approaches such as single-number national reception centres or centres of excellence. Managers will be asked to prepare a plan showing how these examples of best practice could be applied to their organisation. The session will help managers to understand the importance of customer reception and improve the process in their own organisation.

On-line ordering

Communications and information technology has made it much easier for buyer and supplier to communicate with each other. This session introduces managers to current practice and

67

explains the key management tasks in introducing processes such as on-line ordering.

Managers will be asked to prepare an implementation plan for introducing appropriate systems into their organisation.

FREEING PEOPLE FOR CUSTOMER SERVICE

Material world

Customer service includes elements of both personal service and material service. This session explains how the introduction of material service – systems to support customer service processes – can free people to deliver higher standards of personal service. Managers are asked to distinguish the elements of personal and material service in their own organisation and put forward proposals for improving material service. This session will help managers to support front line customer service staff with appropriate systems.

Identikit

This session explains how customer information can help people deliver higher standards of customer service. Managers are introduced to the concept of customer databases, and asked to prepare an outline of the information that they would include in a customer database. The session will help managers make the best use of their existing customer information to improve standards of customer service.

MEASURING CUSTOMER SERVICE PERFORMANCE

Mystery shopper

The quality of customer service is a comparative measure. By comparing one company's customer service performance against another, it is possible to establish benchmarks and aim at being best in the business. This session introduces managers to techniques such as 'mystery shopping' for assessing competitors' performance. Managers are asked to carry out simple field research before the session on a product or service of their choice and report on comparative customer service performance. The session will provide them with a basis for planning research exercises within their own organisation.

69

Customer feedback

Customer feedback is an essential element in any customer service programme. This session will help managers to identify the frequency and type of feedback they need to manage their customer service programmes. Managers are asked to assess the results of a number of fictitious customer responses, review the overall performance and recommend actions to improve performance. The session will help managers to fine-tune their programmes in response to customer needs.

Customer satisfaction

Customer satisfaction is the ultimate measure of any customer service programme, but it is important to know what to measure. This session describes examples of customer satisfaction performance programmes operated by leading public and commercial organisations, and asks delegates to assess whether the correct factors are being measured. Delegates are given guidelines, and asked to develop their own customer satisfaction programme. The session will help managers to understand the importance of continuous improvement in customer satisfaction performance and implement their own programme.

Reward

Customer service and customer satisfaction programmes must recognise the contribution of individual staff or specific departments who have achieved high standards. In this session, managers are asked to identify key people within the organisation who contribute to customer satisfaction, assess their current performance, and develop recognition and incentive programmes to improve performance. The session will help managers understand the importance of motivation and reward in delivering the highest standards of customer service.

70   Who cares wins

This summary session looks at customer service in the context of overall business performance. It provides examples of successful customer service organisations, and asks managers to assess how effective their own customer service policies are. Managers are asked to put together an action plan that focuses on customer service priorities, and to explain how this will improve overall business performance. The session will give managers a broader perspective on the contribution of customer service.

Investing in people

Most of the sessions in this chapter cover management activities rather than personal customer service skills. This session is designed to ensure that managers do not overlook personal skills development. Managers are asked to identify the key skills that they feel should be improved. The session will provide a useful balance and close to a customer service course.

9

Using the salesforce to improve customer service

Introduction

This chapter deals with the changing role of the salesforce – an important factor in determining the success of customer service. The salesforce has been used tactically to maximise sales potential and to 'deal' almost exclusively with the purchasing department. There are a number of important elements in bringing about this change:

- *a shift from short-term sales to managing customer relations;*
- *developing an understanding of the customer's whole business;*
- *acquiring new skills and utilising specialists;*
- *developing a long-term focus;*
- *moving from individual account responsibility to team working;*
- *working at different levels in the customer organisation;*
- *understanding and influencing the complete decision-making structure;*
- *recognising the importance of customer care and customer satisfaction.*

The change in the salesforce's role has been described as 'from hunter to farmer', and it may take more than simple training to achieve this. It is also important to remember that the salesforce does not have individual responsibility in a customer-focused company – everyone has responsibility for maximising customer satisfaction and the support of other people should not be overlooked.

Managing customer relationships

The traditional sales team focus is on sales with a recognition of the importance of profit, but in a customer-focused environment the responsibility is much wider.

- *Is the company delivering the highest standards of satisfaction?*
- *What can we do to build stronger relationships with customers?*

Building customer relationships is a time-consuming process and that can pose problems for sales people who are used to improving sales productivity – achieving the highest levels of turnover for the minimum investment of time. Meeting other decision-makers, reviewing progress on technical projects, making proactive customer care visits, arranging meetings between different members of the account team and briefing other specialists within the company – a traditional sales person would regard these as distractions from the main task of selling.

For years, the pressure has been on to minimise the time spent on travelling or administration to increase sales productivity, and suddenly the salesforce are asked to handle a whole range of other assignments. It is vital that the salesforce understand the importance of these activities and do not regard them as a waste of time.

Understanding customers' whole business

The salesforce must also widen their understanding of the customer's business. In a traditional sales environment, their focus would be on the purchasing department and on the immediate requirement for their products. A customer-focused attitude requires a much broader understanding: what is the customer's business, what are its requirements, how is the company doing, what are the company's success factors, how can we help them to improve their business, what other business opportunities are there apart from current product sales, who needs to be influenced to realise these business opportunities?

This level of business understanding requires a much greater appreciation of business than the basic sales techniques and again the salesforce should not feel they are wasting their time in acquiring this knowledge.

73

From salesforce to account team

The main change for the salesforce is that they are now part of a team dedicated to delivering customer satisfaction. To make the transition to the account team, the salesforce have to acquire a broad range of new skills including project management, communications skills, customer care, presentation skills and team management.

The account support team should be a major contributor to the development of customer focus and the achievement of the highest levels of customer satisfaction. It can also represent a considerable cost factor which requires constant review and enhanced strategies to ensure it adds value to the customer relationship.

There are two main roles within an account team:

- **account support**, which should be focused on the complete service delivered to the customer and maximising customer satisfaction levels;

- **account development**, which should be focused on pre-sales support and the development of the business.

Success factors in customer service delivery

The successful development of the role depends on a number of factors:

- effective working relationships between different members of the team;
- the development of the right skill base to meet the job requirements.

The account manager needs to:

- understand the customer's needs;
- interpret them into product and service requirements;
- ensure the rest of the company understands those requirements;
- deliver a solution that meets those requirements;
- identify and meet future requirements.

The account manager does not need to have an expert knowledge of all those areas; his role is to understand the implications and appoint appropriate specialists to provide the right balance of account skills. The account manager therefore needs a balance of personal and business skills. He must:

- ensure that the customer is presented with a coherent and professional image of the company as a business partner;
- secure a long-term business relationship with the customer as the basis for growing business;
- ensure that the company's solutions are technically sound and based on a proper understanding of the customer's requirements;
- reinforce the customer's perceptions of the benefits of the company's customer focus;

- ensure that the company's total resources are delivered in a way that satisfies customer requirements and supports the objectives of the account plan.

The salesforce and customer satisfaction

The performance of the salesforce can play a key role in achieving high levels of satisfaction. Here are the key tasks.

- *ensure that customer requirements are fully understood and can be met.*
- *Ensure that adequate plans exist within the company to meet customer requirements.*
- *Ensure adequate resource are allocated to achieve the plans.*
- *Monitor the progress of implementation against plans.*
- *Portray a positive image of the company, its products and services in all dealings with the customer.*
- *Ensure the customer is aware his requirements are being met.*

75

The changing role of the salesforce

To succeed in a customer-focused environment, sales staff need to change their role and their attitude. They must become account managers, rather than sales staff. Instead of pursuing short-term profit, they must concentrate on managing customer relationships and they must understand the customer's whole business. Successful account management requires a wide variety of skills, but the good account manager does not need to acquire them all. By co-ordinating the work of specialists, he can achieve key customer service objectives.

10

Communicating priorities to staff

This chapter describes how one company communicated its customer service priorities and tasks to its staff. It shows the importance of researching customer requirements before establishing priorities and ensuring that everyone understands the role they play in delivering customer service. It is based on a staff briefing and includes presentations from a number of senior managers and customer service professionals.

The programme begins with a presentation from a senior executive congratulating staff on their achievements, but encouraging continuous improvement.

EXECUTIVE OVERVIEW

Moving forward with customer service

I am delighted to see that the results of the Customer Satisfaction Index show that we have made real progress in the eyes of our customers. Building and maintaining effective customer relationships is one of the most crucial challenges facing our company, and all our staff deserve congratulations for their contribution to this achievement.

We cannot afford to be complacent, however. Customers' expectations continue to rise and we need to exceed those expectations just to survive as a profitable business. Continuous improvement is essential and therefore every department must develop a flexible customer service action plan that focuses on both the overall priorities and the specific needs of your customers.

We have the service measures to tell us what is happening at national, regional and local level and you should share the findings of these measures with your staff. Customers tell us they want continuity of relationships and effective handovers. They want us to demonstrate an understanding of their business and, if we fail to meet their service expectations, they will almost certainly exercise their choice as consumers.

Make sure that your staff are aware of these findings. Most important, make sure that they are committed to improving every aspect of our customer service performance.

The presentation continues with a look at the headline results from two key measures and a commentary on their implications.

Headline results from the Customer Satisfaction Index

- *Customer satisfaction improved from 65% to 69% nationally*
- *7/8 of the top 10 customer issues are relationship-related*
- *Customers like relationships to be in place for a reasonable length of time*

The headlines from the Customer Satisfaction Index are based on the results of in-depth interviews with customers. The good news is that, nationally, customer satisfaction levels show a real improvement in customers' perceptions of the service they receive from the company. More important, there are improvements in the top three relationship issues:

Contribution to business	+ 3%
Business understanding	+ 3%
Quality of relationship	+ 4%

Those are the issues that customers feel are important and those are the areas that we must concentrate on if we are to strengthen our position even further. The survey also show how customers' perceptions of the importance of different factors are changing. Overall, the results confirm that the quality of relationships remain top of the agenda from the customer's point of view, while pricing and delivery have declined in importance. The table shows the top ten customer issues and you can see how important relationships are.

Current year		Previous year
1	Being supportive of my business	2
2	Understanding my business	3
3	Prices	1
4	Quality of relationship	5
5	Delivery	6
6	Continuity of main account contact	7
7	Quality of account contact	8
8	Accessibility of main account contact	9
9	Speed of carrying out instructions	12
10	Reliable and efficient service	10

The survey gives use a valuable insight into the type and quality of service customers want and it also helps to highlight where we are strong and where we need to improve our performance.

What customers said about our service in the Service Questionnaire

	%	
Headline results	First half	Second half
Overall satisfaction	72	74
Quality of relationships	78	79
Quality of staff	70	71
Quality of service	72	72
Cause to complain	29	27

The recent Service Questionnaire also provides a valuable insight into customers' expectations. Around 60,000 questionnaires were sent out and the results are based on responses in around 22,000 questionnaires returned by customers. As you would expect, there is criticism as well as praise, but the praise helps us to give a first hand impression of the type of service customers expect.

THE IMPORTANCE OF SERVICE MEASURES

The headline results help us focus on the issues that are most important to our customers and we should use those as the basis of our service action plans at every level. Before developing our plans, it is essential that we understand what the service measures are telling us. We use four key indicators that measure service from different perspectives.

The key indicators

Customer Satisfaction Index	provides us with the broad picture and gives us a clear focus for customer service priorities.
Service Questionnaire	measures satisfaction at branch level and is an important indicator of the effectiveness of local relationships.
Complaints Initiative	provides us with the most up to date information on trends and current areas for concern and allows us to react immediately to problems.
Service Performance Index	tests our ability to meet the service standards we set for ourselves and it emphasises the importance of continuous improvement.

80

These four measures provide us with an indicator of how we are performing in the view of our customers.

THE CUSTOMER SATISFACTION INDEX

Focusing on customer priorities

The Customer Satisfaction Index (CSI) helps us to establish the most important service issues and allows us to assess and monitor business customers' perceptions of our performance on each of the key issues. The survey is carried out by an independent business research agency.

This is how it works.
- Customers are independently selected by the agency.
- The agency carries out in-depth telephone interviews with customers to establish their perception of the relative importance of each service issue and the extent to which we are meeting their needs.
- The issues fall into five distinct groups – relationship, transactional, communications, price and delivery.
- The index is calculated using relationship, transactional and communications issues.

- The percentage satisfaction score for each issue is derived by weighting satisfaction against importance.

THE SERVICE QUESTIONNAIRE

Measuring the effectiveness of local relationships

The Service Questionnaire was developed to help individual departments assess the quality of service experienced by their customers. It is also an effective way of communicating our commitment to service, and feedback from customers indicates that they welcome the opportunity to comment. Here is how it works.

- Customers are selected by the departments.
- A questionnaire, covering letter and prepaid reply envelope are mailed to each customer.
- After initial examination, the completed questionnaires are forwarded to an agency for processing.
- Participating departments receive summary reports which provide a detailed analysis of their performance and a comparison with the national average.

81

THE COMPLAINTS INITIATIVE

Learning from complaints

Complaints can be a positive benefit to our business – provided they are handled effectively. Complaints act as a warning sign that we are not meeting our customers' expectations, and they are often the first indication that customers are unhappy and may be considering moving their business. Unfortunately, many complaints are not even recognised and therefore are not acknowledged or resolved until it is too late. However, research in other fields indicates that customers who have their complaints resolved are likely to express high levels of satisfaction.

The Complaints Initiative was introduced to provide a systematic, consistent approach to handling complaints throughout the company and it offers a number of important benefits.

- It helps staff recognise when customers are complaining, how they complain and how the complaint can be resolved.
- It helps staff identify the root causes of complaints and appropriate corrective action.

This is how the initiative operates:

- When a complaint has been identified, a Complaint Action Form is completed and forwarded to the appropriate area for action and follow-up.

- Each complaint is allocated a code to help identify and group particular issues. The forms are collated and checked by the co-ordinator and a copy is forwarded to an agency.

- Departments receive monthly reports showing the percentage of complaints for each code for the previous month and the period to date. The report also provides a comparison of results at national level.

SERVICE PERFORMANCE INDEX

An independent assessment of service levels

The Service Performance Index is used to independently assess our levels of service and measure progress against the standards set out in our corporate guidelines. This programme is important because, over time, our customers' expectations rise and we have to meet and exceed those expectations to attract and retain customers.

The index uses three techniques – the Point-of-Sale Initiative, the Telephone Initiative and Mystery Shopping, the most important technique which constitutes 70 per cent of the index. This is how the Mystery Shopper programme works.

- Selected departments receive personal enquiries and telephone calls monthly, together with four personal visits per year.
- After the visit, the mystery shopper completes an audit sheet, sends one copy to the department and one to a central agency for collation.
- The agency produces summary reports detailing the overall score and individual standards.

The presentation then goes on to look at the way the service measures can be used to establish priorities within the company.

COMMUNICATING SERVICE

Stress the importance of service

It is vital that staff understand the importance of customer service. The success of customer-focused organisations like British Airways, Virgin, Marks & Spencer and Kwik-Fit is well documented. These companies not only achieve high levels of customer satisfaction, they are profitable too.

Studies by the Strategic Planning Institute have identified that companies with superior quality as perceived by their customers are on average four times more profitable than companies with inferior quality. Conversely, poor service not only leads to dissatisfied customers, it costs money.

Service is the single most important factor in distinguishing our company from competitors and it is for this reason that quality of service has been retained as one of the three key business objectives alongside profit before tax and profit after tax. Staff must understand that sales and service go hand-in-hand. We build sales by meeting customers' needs and developing long-term relationships with them. If service is poor, it is unlikely that customers will continue to buy from us.

83

Everyone must realise that customer service is not the responsibility of a few individuals, quality service is everyone's concern.

Focus on the priorities

The service measures provide a broad view of the way customers perceive our service and also give us a specific indication of what our customers feel. This information is vital to developing an action plan by providing a clear picture of the strengths and weaknesses of individual departments. When you review the results of those measures with your staff, compare them with the broad picture identified in the Customer Satisfaction Index. Ask staff to assess how they feel their department is performing relative to the rest of the company and ask them to identify the areas where they feel improvements are most needed.

DEVELOP A PLAN

Good planning is a key factor in improving customer service and the Service Action Plan will help to focus on the activities that will improve branch service performance by building on strengths and eliminating weaknesses. It is important that you do not try to take on too much and that your goals are realistic and achievable. These are the important factors in developing your plan.

- Use the service measures to identify priorities, concentrating specifically on relationship issues.
- Set specific, achievable objectives.
- Concentrate on continuous small manageable improvements.
- Involve staff in developing ideas and implementing solutions
- Make use of the Service Action Plan.

PUT QUALITY SERVICE INTO ACTION

As you saw in our review of the Service Questionnaire and the Customer Satisfaction Index, building and maintaining effective customer relationships is one of the most crucial challenges facing our company. In any face-to-face meeting, telephone conversation or correspondence, the individual member of staff is the company to the customer. Improving our standards of customer service is vital because it represents durable competitive advantage and the reward is increased, market-leading profits.

84

CONTINUITY IS AS VITAL AS SERVICE QUALITY

Although we made good progress in relationship issues, one area we should not overlook is continuity of relationships. In both the Service Questionnaire and the Customer Satisfaction Index, customers expressed concern about the impact of personnel changes on their business relationships. Customers feel that continuity is important and, although we may not be able to avoid change, we can minimise risk by handling the change professionally and efficiently.

IMPROVING SERVICE PERFORMANCE

The review shows that we have achieved progress but we must continue to maintain our standards and aim for even higher levels of customer satisfaction in the coming year. Customer satisfaction has improved, we have the programmes and the processes to improve our service even further, customers have told us they value long-term relationships with their bank, and our profit performance shows that quality customer service brings positive results. Let's make sure we really capitalise on our strengths in the new year.

11

The customer service process

The first part of this book has looked at the background issues in delivering quality customer service. It should help you concentrate on having the right people in position and developing the right customer service skills. The second part of the book looks at the way in which customer service can be used to improve the various processes that occur between an organisation and its customers.

Quality contact is important at every stage from initial enquiry through pre-sales advice to aftercare and this can help to build the highest levels of customer satisfaction.

Making it easy for customers to contact you

Customers who find it difficult to contact an organisation are unlikely to remain customers for long. However, there are a number of low-cost options for simplifying contact including fax, answerphone, longer opening hours, freephone, freepost, reply-paid cards and other techniques. Customers will save time in placing orders or making enquiries and this can improve satisfaction levels.

Helping customers make the right choice

Customer service begins before the sale when customers are

making decisions about a product or service. By providing the right level of information, advice and guidance, a company can build high levels of customer satisfaction, even before a sale takes place. Customers will feel more confident that they have made the right choice and this helps to build long-term loyalty.

Make it convenient for customer to do business

Is your business conveniently located? Is there adequate customer parking? Do your opening hours suit your customers? Is it easy to find your department? Can you introduce other changes that make it more convenient for customers to do business? Research has shown that convenience is a major factor in selecting retail outlets. By making it convenient for your customers you can help to build a sure foundation for business.

Improve customer reception

When customers telephone or make personal contact, it is important that their calls are handled efficiently. There are a number of techniques for improving performance, such as setting up customer files so that full buying or service history as well as customer details are available to staff who handle enquiries. You can also establish processes for routing enquiries to the right contact or offering to call the customer back if the right contact is not available.

Replying to enquiries within agreed timescales

When customers make enquiries, they expect a reasonably prompt response. To ensure that enquiries are handled efficiently, managers should set time standards for different activities. For example, a request for quotation should be met within x hours; delivery of a spare part within y days; letters of complaint should be processed within x days. It is important to identify critical processes and ensure that they carry time standards.

Keep customers informed on progress at all times

If customers are waiting for an urgent delivery or for a service call, research shows that they like to be kept informed on progress. There are a number of scenarios where progress calls can help to reassure customers and demonstrate high levels of customer care.

Follow up sales quickly

87

A courtesy call or letter to a customer who has just bought from you is a proactive form of customer service. There are a number of techniques for following up sales and standard letters and questionnaires can be used as part of the process.

Use complaints in a positive way

Customer complaints can be used to measure the health of an organisation and to highlight areas for improvement. By using a positive technique for recording and responding to customer complaints and implementing improvement programmes, a company can demonstrate that it recognises and respects customer concerns.

Set up procedures for handling problems

Customer complaints or other customer service problems must

be handled at the right level. In some cases, front line staff can be given the authority to deal with the majority of problems but there should also be procedures for escalating a problem to a higher level of management if it cannot be resolved satisfactorily.

Offer customers a helpline

Advice and guidance can help customers to deal with problems or queries. A properly manned helpline can help to improve customer service by providing operating tips or timely advice if there are problems.

Improving the efficiency of administration

Poor service at the checkout, inaccurate invoicing or other forms of administrative inefficiency can destroy the benefits of other forms of customer service. These are high-risk areas because the functions are usually carried out by people who are not directly in contact with customers.

Highlighting the critical processes

This brief overview of the customer contact process shows that there are many opportunities to improve customer relationships. By examining the ways in which your company deals with its customers, you can identify the critical processes where you can focus attention and improve performance in areas that are important to customers.

12

Make it easy for customers to contact you

How often have you tried to get through to a company and found that their lines are busy or they are closed or they are located in an inconvenient place? Customers who find it difficult to contact an organisation are unlikely to remain customers for long.

This section looks at ways in which you can help your customers do business by making it easier for them to buy from you. Many companies put up artificial barriers to trade by making their ordering procedures complex, failing to provide adequate product information or setting up complex procedures for billing. This section describes a number of techniques that will help your customers to select, order and obtain products easily.

Telephone or postal response?

First, decide what action your prospects are to take:

- **placing an order;**
- **requesting a sales call;**
- **requesting further information.**

The following examples show how response mechanisms can be used.

- **Improving customer care**
  A fast-food chain offered customers a freephone number to give their comments on quality of service and make general enquiries. This improved customer care and halved the cost of handling customer complaints.

- **Instant product information**
  Manufacturers who want to simplify distribution of product information include a FastFax number on their direct marketing material. Prospects request information and it is faxed back quickly.

Options for response

You should also review the cost, convenience and practicality of the response options; they are:

- *Postal-based response mechanisms*:
  (i)   reply-paid cards;
  (ii)   reply-paid envelopes;
  (iii) freepost addresses;

- *Telephone-based response mechanisms*:
  (i)   freephone 0800 numbers which are free;
  (ii)   Lo-call 0345 numbers which only cost callers local rates;
  (iii) 0891 numbers which cost a specified amount;

- *Fax-based mechanisms*:
  (i)   Freefax 0800 numbers which are free;
  (ii)   FastFax services which provide specified product information at normal call rates.

Which option is right?

- Research carried out by the Direct Mail Information Service indicates that consumers felt more comfortable with postal reply mechanisms because they allow more time for consideration and there is no sales pressure.

- Business reply is regarded as more suitable for business and financial mailings.

- Freepost is regarded as a 'friendly' mechanism.

- Telephone-based services are more immediate and can be more personal. The 0891 information service numbers can be used to provide useful customer information and generate revenue.

- Freefax numbers allow standard printed information to be distributed rapidly to callers with fax machines.

24-hour communications

If the telephones are not manned around the clock, how can you ensure that customers can reach your company? There are a number of options:

- installing answering machines so that customers can always leave messages;

- providing mobile phone or home telephone numbers;

- using a telephone answering bureau to handle your calls outside hours.

Dealing with customer enquiries

Simplifying customer access can improve customer convenience. By creating a central contact point for all customer enquiries, you can ensure that every incoming customer contact is handled efficiently.

This is particularly appropriate for companies who have a number of separate locations or who are organised by product group. At an enquiry centre all incoming calls are handled by a central receptionist and routed to the appropriate specialist. The customer does not have to waste time trying to track down the right contact. The enquiry centre should handle incoming calls for queries such as:

91

- product information;
- technical information;.
- service requests;
- literature;
- complaints;
- estimates and ordering;
- delivery;
- accounts.

Many of these calls would be routed direct to the appropriate department, but an increasing number of companies are making the receptionist responsible for customer contact and incident management.

For example, if an important customer makes a service request, the receptionist takes the basic details and arranges for a specialist to call the customer back within an agreed timescale. The receptionist may go further and maintain contact with the customer until the service problem has been resolved. The process is known as incident management and helps to reassure the customer that appropriate action is being taken.

The enquiry centre is a valuable method of ensuring that the customer receives a consistent standard of quality service on every contact.

Product information

Clear up-to-date product information is vital to effective customer relationships. The marketing communications specialists on your team should take responsibility for managing the quality of all product information, including:

- technical literature;
- catalogues;
- technical updates;
- product proposals.

Simplifying ordering

Ordering costs both supplier and purchaser money, so anything that can simplify the ordering process will save your customers money and improve customer relationships.

Taking the initiative

Many companies who sell fast-moving products such as spare parts operate what they call the 'ring-round'. Every day sales staff contact the customer to see if they need next day delivery or anything more urgent. Often the customer will not need to place an immediate order, but still appreciates the convenience of having that daily reminder.

Telephone/fax ordering

Routine purchases can be ordered over the telephone or by fax. To make it even more convenient for customers, answering machines or 24-hour fax machines mean that the customer can place orders whenever it is convenient.

On-line ordering

With the growth in computerised manufacturing and stock control systems, companies are using on-line ordering to simplify administration. A motor dealership with a number of regional branches used on-line ordering to speed up and simplify their parts ordering procedures.

Branch staff were able to access the central parts department computer over public communications networks; they could get immediate information on the stock available of various parts and place their orders. Stock levels were automatically adjusted and the system produced delivery notes, invoices and packing instructions. This process cut out several layers of paperwork and speeded up ordering and delivery.

The on-line ordering process can be extended to key customers with its logical conclusion in the Ford system described earlier.

On-line systems depend on effective communications links between supplier and buyer; companies can either set up their own dedicated networks or utilise public networks.

Customised administration

If your customer is buying a large number of separate items from you, you can simplify their administrative burden in a number of ways:

(a) providing 'single line' invoices for groups of different purchases;

(b) integrating your accounts system with theirs so that they receive financial information in a compatible format;

(c) using electronic data interchange to reduce paperwork.

Summary

Making it easier for your customers to buy by using services such as freephone or freepost is a sure way of improving customer satisfaction. Communications make it easier for your key customers to obtain up-to-date commercial and delivery information. Providing your customers with a single point of access for all enquiries makes it easier for them to do business and allows you to control the quality of customer contact.

13

Help customers make the right choice

Customer service begins before the sale, when customers are making a decision about a product or service. By providing the right level of information, advice and guidance, you can build high levels of customer satisfaction, even before the sale takes place.

How can you make sure that customers have all the information they need to choose the right product or service? You could just rely on sending them product literature. If they need more information, offer them a telephone helpline. If your company is selling more sophisticated products or services, you may need to provide more detailed briefings and information packs.

Using product literature

In Chapter 7, we saw from the example of the civil servant who took early retirement, and wanted to know where to invest his lump sum payment, that he preferred the institution that tailored its response to his needs as an individual. Chapter 7 gives various methods of finding out more about the customer's needs and thus ensuring that this approach works.

Provide advice over a helpline

Increasing numbers of companies are providing customers and

prospects with a freephone helpline, and encouraging them to make enquiries about products and services over the helpline. The helplines are manned by specialists who combine technical knowledge with an ability to talk to individuals at the right level – callers are not intimidated by talking to people who reply in jargon. The staff talk about the customer's needs – how do you plan to use the product, what results do you want, how often do you use it? They concentrate on identifying the customer's needs, not doing a sales pitch on their products.

Staff are encouraged to develop a relationship over the phone, not deal with queries as quickly as possible and meet a daily target. Dialogue and a relaxed attitude help to build customer confidence. The customer who gets honest, straightforward answers will trust the company. Helplines build a relationship before the selling starts. Once you have established customer needs, your sales team can concentrate on offering the right product. The result – customer satisfaction at every stage. You'll find more information on helplines in Chapter 21.

96

Helping business customers make decisions

When business customers make decisions about high-value products and services, they may need more information and guidance than literature or a helpline can provide.

You can use the skills and knowledge within your organisation or department to help the customer make the right decision. Improving your customer's skills in areas of complexity and uncertainty demonstrates high levels of professionalism and customer care. By working with customers to improve their skills at a strategic level, you can improve working relationships.

Executive briefings

Executive briefings can be used to help clients develop a more informed approach to decision-making. Telecommunications specialists run briefing sessions for telecommunications managers and senior executives at venues around the country. The intention is to ensure that customers make the right decisions about telecommunications systems.

The engineering business contains many examples of companies who help their clients to make informed decisions about new materials or new processes. Although executive briefings are predominantly found in high-technology businesses, they can be equally applied to the service sector and to any activity where the purchasing decision is complex.

When executive briefing is important

A number of scenarios can be used to identify opportunities for introducing customer briefings.

- *Customers have to make fundamental decisions about the future direction of their business.* The new product or service will have a significant impact on the future direction of their business, and it is important that customers understand the full implications. Purchasing is not simply a matter of replacing an existing product or service, or changing suppliers, it will reshape the business. Customers will have to reconsider how their future product range will shape up, what markets they can enter and how they will manage their business in the new environment.

- *The product or service will have an impact on the organisational structure or working practices.* New manufacturing techniques, new materials or new technology could require a fundamental change in working practice. The customer will not be making a strategic change in direction, but will be doing the same things in a different way. It is essential that the management team understand how they will have to change their organisation to take advantage of the new developments. Failure to change means that they may only partially benefit. The change could involve retraining or new investment or reorganisation.

- *The product or service is based on a new technology and the customer has no experience of assessing its cost effectiveness.* New technology could offer major benefits but cost more initially. The management team may dismiss the product or service as too expensive but not realise the full cost implications. A briefing session could help them to understand the full through-life implications which may benefit the company. Briefing sessions would help them to assess the product from a different point of view.

- *The product or service is part of a complete solution that provides broad-ranging business benefits for the customer.* It is vital for the supplier to explain how all the elements of the package work together.

- *New legislation will have an impact on the customer and the supplier provides a product or service that will help customers meet requirements.* The company's expertise can help the customer to understand the implications of the legislation and develop a strategy for dealing with it.

- *The supplier has skills that the customer wishes to acquire.* Skills and knowledge transfer are an important part of executive briefing.

- *A supplier wishes to demonstrate professionalism.* Executive briefing centres can help to position a company as an expert in a specific product or service area, building closer relationships with clients.

- *Consultancy is an important part of the total product and service package;* briefing sessions are an integral part of the consultancy process.

- *A company wants to build partnership with key customers and uses the briefing sessions to build a better understanding of the customer's business processes.*

The briefing process

Seminars

At a seminar, a number of speakers make presentations to the audience and may participate in question and answer sessions. The audience can be invited to a 'closed' event, or may choose to attend an 'open' event. The seminar can be a self-contained event or it may form part of a wider event such as an exhibition or conference. You may be one of a number of companies presenting at the seminar – the other presenters may include your competitors – or you may limit the presenters to people from your own organisation. The more control you have over the event and the presenters, the more you can influence the response and attitudes of the audience.

However, it may be more appropriate to present your message within the context of an independent, authoritative seminar where your presentation will be seen as impartial.

99

In deciding what form the seminar should take, you should consider the following.

- *Will the audience include the types of company and the target audience you want to reach*? If you are inviting delegates, you decide the audience, but if the seminar is open, you need to know who the organisers are targeting.

- *Does the seminar have a theme and programme that corresponds with the values of your customer focus programme*? For example, an open seminar on 'Manufacturing in the 90s' would be appropriate for an engineering company which wished to reach key manufacturing decision-makers.

- *Does the seminar have the right degree of authority*? If the manufacturing seminar was organised by an official body such as the Department of Trade and Industry, that would add a degree of authority to the presenting companies.

- *Do the other seminar presentations complement your message and reinforce your theme*"?

- *Will the seminar format provide you with enough time to*

present your arguments in detail? If not, how easily can you follow up the seminar audience?

There are a number of important actions you should take to ensure that the seminar meets your communications objectives:

- *Set specific objectives for the seminar, for example, to raise awareness of the importance of your proposal.*
- *Select speakers with the authority and status to present strategic messages.*
- *Ensure that the presentation focuses on concerns and business issues that are important to your customers.*
- *Incorporate the positioning messages that stress the strategic benefits of working with your company.*

100

Using the example of the fictitious 'Manufacturing in the 90s' seminar, this is an example of how an engineering company might utilise the seminar to reach key contacts in industry.

Manufacturing in the 90s

'Manufacturing in the 90s' is run by an independent conference organiser in conjunction with a government body such as the Department of Trade and Industry. The organisers have assembled a group of presenters from industry, government and the academic world and have invited an audience of senior executives from Britain's leading manufacturing companies. The speakers cover strategically important topics such as new developments in manufacturing technology, the importance of information systems, changing investment criteria and the human resource implications of the likely changes.

Within the context of the seminar, a presentation on the strategic benefits of partnership is appropriate and helps to provide senior executives with a broad perspective. The seminar positions partnership as an integral element of competitive manufacturing management. The company's paper is presented by the managing director and provides a unique opportunity for high-level contact with other senior executives.

After the seminar, the company takes the opportunity to maintain communication by mailing management summaries of the seminar papers to delegates and important customers or prospects who were unable to attend. Telephone research conducted before and after the seminar revealed that awareness of the benefits of partnership had increased by 18 per cent, and this provided a valuable basis for planning the next stage of the communications programme.

Executive briefings

Executive briefings are similar in many ways to seminars, but they are completely under your control. For example, the briefings can adopt the same format as a seminar, with a number of different speakers from your company presenting on related topics. However, the content of the presentations is completely under your control and can be tailored to the business needs of individual customers.

A number of larger organisations have set up special executive briefing centres to concentrate on this important aspect of business development. The briefing centres are often located in converted country houses with full presentation facilities, accommodation, catering and areas for discussion and relaxation. The intention is to create an environment where busy executives can get away from day-to-day pressures and concentrate on issues of strategic importance.

101

An environment like that is helpful, but not essential. Management briefings can be held on your customers' premises, at your offices or in a conference-type location such as a hotel or business centre. It is however important to provide an area where the meeting can take place without disturbance in an atmosphere that is conducive to strategic thinking.

The briefing is designed to bring executives up to date with issues that are seen as important to their business and to help them decide how to assess the potential of an issue such as partnership within their organisation. The agenda for an executive briefing on partnership might include the following sessions.

The business benefits of partnership.

How is partnership currently used within the industry?

Is partnership relevant to your organisation?

The management implications of partnership.

Assessing the potential for partnership.

A timetable and action programme for implementing partnership.

As well as demonstrating your understanding of your customer's business and your willingness to help them improve their business performance, a briefing session can encourage open discussion on your customers' business needs and improve working relationships. The executive briefing gives your customers the opportunity to decide whether they can work comfortably with you and demonstrates that partnership depends on close working relationships and an atmosphere of trust.

To help customers get the optimum benefit from executive briefings, provide them with workbooks, case histories and models to use in planning their own programmes.

Management reports

Management reports can be issued to different members of the target audience to explain complex issues and outline the main topics customers should review. Many management reports are based on market research and provide customers with an overview of current practice. A management report is not a promotional publication. It should be written in a neutral tone and it should offer customers objective advice that will help them to make effective decisions by improving the quality of the decision-making process, you can ensure that your proposals are evaluated professionally. Management reports demonstrate that you understand your own and your partner's business and that you are prepared to help your customers improve the quality of their own decision-making.

An information systems company produced a management report on the management implications of Just-In-Time (JIT) manufacturing processes to ensure that their customers were aware of their own responsibilities. Research had shown that companies who adopted JIT, without considering the full potential impact on their business, tended to blame their information systems for problems that were actually due to lack of understanding and poor management.

The management report was structured as a briefing document for different members of the management team. It explained that the JIT approach to manufacturing required the commitment and involvement of the whole management team. JIT decisions were shown to be wide-ranging, involving the chief executive and board director, together with managers and executives responsible for production, finance, purchasing and marketing. The report explained the potential benefits of JIT, illustrating them with statistics and conclusions from the information system manufacturer's experience in implementing JIT in its own factories. The report then outlined an agenda for discussing JIT and highlighted the critical management decisions. The report was widely used in manufacturing industry and was adopted as a standard by a number of professional institutes who were trying to improve management standards.

103

Management reports play an important role in building effective relations with contacts at all levels in the customer organisation by promoting informed, thorough discussion of the potential of issues facing the customer.

- *They demonstrate to senior executives that your proposals have taken their business issues into consideration.*
- *They help middle managers to make informed decisions about key business issues and thus reduce the risk of poor decision-making that is narrowly focused.*
- *They can help purchasing executives to take a broader view of the importance of a proposal by demonstrating the wide-ranging implications and business benefits that can result.*

Summary

Giving customers the right amount of information before a sale can help to build customer satisfaction from the outset. The information can be provided in the form of literature, telephone advice or more sophisticated techniques such as seminars, management briefings or management reports.

14

Make it convenient for customers to do business

Is your business conveniently located? Is there adequate customer parking? Do your opening hours suit your customers? Can you introduce other changes that make it more convenient for your customers to do business? What about selling direct to the public rather than going through intermediaries? How can you use the telephone to sell or conduct business? If you put barriers in the way of customers, you can be certain that they will look for easier alternatives.

When the Post Office relocated some of its main branches away from traditional town centre sites to out-of-town retail developments or into other central retail sites, it was criticised for changing a long-standing service, but it was able to counter that criticism by pointing out that it had improved convenience for a wide range of domestic and business users, as well as taking the opportunity to benefit from the introduction of new services and new technology.

This chapter looks at ways of improving convenience for the customer and uses examples mainly from the retail sector. Longer opening hours, more convenient locations, better parking or public transport links and integration of leisure and shopping activities have helped to make shopping a more convenient experience.

However, the same principles can be applied to business and service industries: components manufacturers, for example, who locate their factories in close proximity to key customers so that both can enjoy the benefits of closer working relationships, or the example of Eastern Electricity who make their customer help centre available 24 hours a day for any type of enquiry. The intention in all cases is to make it as easy as possible for customers to use the service. Automatic teller machines make banking and building society services available 24 hours a day while 'open all hours' corner shops enjoy a powerful neighbourhood competitive advantage over traditional shops.

Why should you look at the convenience of your service?

106 The convenience approach can be valuable in a number of business scenarios.

- Your company is losing business to competitors who offer more convenient forms of service, longer opening hours or a more convenient location.

- Your company wishes to attract a broader audience who are not able to use the service in its current form – car service customers, for example, who use their cars throughout the week are offered Saturday service or overnight service, or service at the local rail station car park.

- Your company wants to make convenience a major selling platform – for example offering customers a no-appointment-necessary service or 24-hour opening so that customers can use the service whenever they need to.

- Your customers are demanding better standards of service and their needs can be used to develop and operate customer focus standards.

- The opportunity exists to introduce higher standards of customer service by taking advantage of new technology or new facilities – for example by relocating a factory to take advantage of Just-In-Time techniques.

- Convenience is identified as the most important factor in customer research.

How the Post Office improved convenience

When the Post Office was carrying out a review of its strategy for main branch location, it carried out research into customer needs and changing retail patterns. Many of the main post offices were located in central high street areas with sub-post offices located in neighbourhoods to provide a local service. The main post offices provided a wider range of services and were the key to the Post Office's future development. Sub-post offices provided essential Royal Mail, payment and savings facilities but did not offer the broader range of services.

Future developments would require a greater use of technology and would put a different emphasis on space utilisation with the development of post shops and other special retailing activities within the Post Office. In many cases, the traditional sites did not have the potential for conversion or expansion, and this would limit future change and growth. The opportunity to rebuild or relocate in traditional town centre areas was also difficult because of the property costs.

More important, consumer habits were changing. Traffic congestion, parking restrictions and a reduction in public transport made it more difficult for customers to make a quick visit to the Post Office – the visit would have to be part of a wider shopping trip. Customers were also making extensive use of out-of-town shopping centres where all the important food and retail outlets were to be found with easy access by car and public transport.

Although the Post Office recognised the potential consumer benefits of relocation in terms of improving customer service and convenience, it was also aware of its responsibilities to specific groups within the community, particularly the elderly or people who would not be able to get to the new locations easily by private or public transport.

107

The Post Office was seen as abandoning its traditional role and there was a concern amongst local opinion-formers that this was a change in direction. As part of the development programme, the Post Office undertook a process of local consultation and information to ensure that their proposals were fully acceptable. A briefing pack for local opinion-formers, aimed at politicians, local councillors, trade associations and consumer groups explained the overall benefits.

- The new branches would have better parking facilities and would be located close to public transport.
- Opening hours would be longer and the branches would provide a wider range of services.
- The new offices would offer other convenience facilities, including larger counter areas, a more open aspect, disabled access and facilities such as telephones and photobooths.
- In many cases the post offices were located within a store and operated as a franchise. The store owner would provide the facilities and the staff who would be trained in Post Office procedures and wear Post Office uniforms. The Post Office within a store was seen as an important customer benefit, cutting down the number of separate shopping visits a customer had to make and offering the advantages of one-stop shopping.
- Many of the new post offices would incorporate new technology which would allow the Post Office to deliver higher standards of service and deliver a wider range of services.

Making shopping more convenient

The same process of convenience can be applied to the retail sector. A regional shopping centre like Lakeside in Essex reflects all the aspects of convenience. The centre is located close to the M25 motorway network and the Dartford crossing, making access easy from London and the Home Counties. Local customers have fast access routes through dual carriageways, special access roads and effective public transport. The centre is built on a large site with adequate free parking and contains all the most popular retail outlets under one roof with covered access to all large and small stores.

Refreshments are available throughout the centre and entertainments, in the form of cinemas and other leisure activities, are an integral part of the centre so that groups or families can use the centre for different purposes. Larger specialist superstores for electrical goods, carpets, computers, toys and other consumer durables are located on an adjacent retail centre, extending the concept of one-stop shopping. The stores feature longer opening hours and many make use of the latest electronic point-of-sale facilities to ensure that shopping is convenient and easy.

109

Using the telephone to improve convenience and personal service

When First Direct introduced round-the-clock telephone banking, it was a breakthrough in customer service. Customers enjoy a personal service whenever they choose to do business and they can carry out transactions without visiting a branch. First Direct utilised the power of the telephone to improve personal service.

Many customers of traditional high street banks felt that they were simply account numbers and that personal service was a thing of the past. First Direct focused clearly on what it saw were the customers' real needs – a personal service at a convenient time for the customer, with a high degree of flexibility. The concept was simple – 24-hour banking by telephone. A customer rang up at any time and was able to carry out a wide range of transactions over the telephone. Far from being an impersonal telephone service, the First Direct contact was perceived as a friendly and personal service where the customer was treated as an individual, rather than a number.

Selling services direct to the public

There is a parallel in the insurance business where companies had traditionally maintained a field force of collectors and agents calling on households. Direct debits and other forms of automated payment enabled the insurance company to reduce their overheads but lose vital contact.

Direct Line Insurance carved out a profitable niche in the car insurance market by offering customers a highly efficient tele-sales and claims handling operation. Rather than contact a broker or a traditional insurance company direct the customer was able to benefit from a professional, no-frills operation. By reducing its overheads and not having to support a salesforce or a branch network, the company was able to offer an extremely competitive service. When prospects called, any enquiry was handled by trained sales staff who worked through a planned sequence of questions to ensure the customer received an accurate quote. The quote was handled on computer and was immediate. If the customer accepted the quote, the policy was immediately put into effect and no further action was needed.

Claims were handled in the same straightforward way. The customer phoned in, described the incident and the claim would be dealt with rapidly. This standard of service enabled Direct Line to show good profits and set a standard that other insurance companies tried to follow.

How the direct approach can be used

The 'direct' approach is now being found in a number of other markets and it can be used to meet different scenarios.

- Customers carry out specific transactions which do not depend on specialist skills.

- Computers provide all the customer information necessary to carry out transactions. Customer details are held on personal computer and can be accessed by any member of the telephone team.

- The customer sees convenience as an important aspect of the service and this convenience is not available through other forms of service delivery. In this case, customers would have to visit a branch, and they may not have time or the location could be difficult.

- The service can be positioned as prompt, flexible and personal and can be tailored to the needs of individual customers.

- Quality of personal service is seen as more important than location.

- People and resources can be concentrated in specific areas, rather than scattered around a branch network.

- The service does not have to be located in a particular area and it does not have to be situated near the mechanism for delivering the service; for example, telephone banking does not require a high street location.

Improving convenience in your organisation

- *Research and identify the convenience factors customers feel are most important.*

- *Establish a set of customer focus standards for the new service.*

- *Consult customers and other influencers if significant change is involved.*

- *Identify the staff training requirements to ensure that customers receive the highest standards of service.*

- *Assess the potential of new technology to improve conve-*

111

nience further.

- *Look for opportunities to introduce new services or products that take advantage of the new facilities.*
- *Can you substitute a direct telephone-based service for any of your customer-facing sales operations?*
- *What are the key customer requirements for such a service?*
- *How would the change impinge on customers?*
- *Could the telephone-based service be integrated with traditional services?*
- *What are the main skills requirements?*

Summary

112

This chapter has looked at ways of improving convenience for the customer and shown how companies in the retail sector have used factors such as longer opening hours, more convenient locations, better parking or public transport links, and integration of leisure and shopping activities to make shopping a more convenient experience. The same principles can be applied to business and service industries by building closer working relationships and making it easier for customers to do business. In many cases, new technology can be used to improve aspects of convenience or to launch new services that help attract a different audience.

15

Improve customer reception

'If you make it easy for customers to contact you, you'll soon develop closer relationships, but put barriers in their way, and they'll just try the next number on their list.'

According to the marketing director of a mail order company, effective telephone reception is proving to be a vital element in quality customer service.

Profiting from customer calls

If your business receives a high volume of incoming calls – sales, information or service queries, bookings or transaction processing – you need to ensure that those calls are answered quickly and efficiently. A quality response not only enhances customer service, it is the key to increased revenue and profit.

Developments in telecommunications technology mean that sophisticated response systems are no longer the preserve of large corporations. Systems are now available to small and medium-sized businesses that can transform the quality of customer response. The key is call centres, as this telecommunications consultant explains.

'By concentrating your telephone specialists in call centres, supervising their performance, and using a technique known as Automatic Call Distribution (ACD), you can ensure that

calls are answered quickly and efficiently, with the optimum use of staff time and telephone lines.'

A small engineering company recently invested in a call centre system to handle sales order processing and provide customers with a technical helpline service. Although they had offered telephone support in the past, the service had been hampered by poor call-handling techniques. At peak times, customers would wait several minutes to get through and were sometimes transferred to extensions that were unmanned. The customer's perception was shaped by the call response not by the service that was eventually delivered.

The system they installed uses a range of computerised tools to monitor performance and improve control over call response. Information on the status of telephone lines and groups of call centre staff shows what is happening to calls as they come in and allows the supervisor to manage operations efficiently. The system also includes features such as call queuing and call prioritisation to ensure that the call centre operates cost-effectively and delivers high levels of customer satisfaction.

The engineering company found that the system allowed them to handle the same volume of calls more efficiently but, more important, it allowed them to keep customers informed even while they were waiting. User-friendly queuing techniques are used to ensure that calls are answered in sequence and no calls go unanswered. All incoming calls are queued and answered in order and the system can be programmed to feed calls to waiting receptionists or specific named individuals automatically.

- Calls are automatically routed to the receptionist in a group who has been free the longest.
- If all the receptionists in a group are busy, calls can overflow to a second group.
- Calls can be routed to other groups after a preset ringing time.

You may already have a call centre in your organisation but, if not, look closely at your business to see if there are opportunities to improve the speed and quality of call response. Call centres are particularly appropriate for the following activities:

- enquiry and help desks;
- telemarketing;
- financial services ;
- retail or wholesale order entry;
- reservation systems;
- customer service departments.

By monitoring the length of time it takes for incoming calls to be answered and assessing the workload on different members of staff, you can plan a call centre that meets your business needs. These are some of the important factors to consider:

115

- *What type of calls should the centre handle – orders, enquiries, help, service?*
- *Should it be a central facility or based in different regions?*
- *What is the target call response time – how long can you keep callers waiting?*
- *How many staff and how many lines will be needed to handle planned volumes within the target response times?*

Networking facilities allow multi-site companies to operate a single call centre; customers call their local branch, but the call is re-directed automatically to the call centre. A distributed call centre network means that callers can overflow to remote sites in peak periods or be diverted to specialist centres of excellence in different sites.

These network options increase flexibility and can be used to enhance customer service even further. Many systems allow you to link computer and business applications to your telephone operations. For example, the integration of screen-based customer information can help to improve productivity and customer service on call response. To maximise the benefits of the call centre, agents can make outbound sales calls or enquiries when incoming traffic is low. For increased productivity, outbound calls can be generated from a database with integrated call information available on screen.

Although the use of call handling systems is not new, the technology is now more accessible and it is being increasingly used by small and medium-sized organisations in the public and private sector. It can provide the basis for a highly efficient telephone-based customer contact system, and research shows that effective contact is a key factor in achieving the highest levels of customer satisfaction.

Effective reception works in any business. It makes the customer feel welcome, demonstrates commitment to customer service and provides the opportunity to add value and increase business.

116

Making the most of your service records

When a regular customer calls you to place an order or service request, how do your staff respond? Do they waste the customer's time asking for basic details or do they make the customer feel important by having all the information to hand?

Here is an example of a customer receptionist who has used service records to make a customer feel special.

Garage	Good morning, London Motors. How can we help?
Customer	I'd like the service department please.
Garage	Certainly, sir, could I take your name and registration please. Thank you, Mr Jones, I'll put you through to Brian, the service receptionist who dealt with you last time you called.
Garage	Hello, Mr Jones, how is the GTi? Has it been running OK since we tuned it last month?
Customer	Yes, it's been its old self again. I was actually calling about the brakes. I think they might need attention.

Garage   You're probably right, we check them on the regular service, but the last time we changed the pads was two years ago and you've done more than 25,000 miles since then. We'll have a look at those for you.

Customer   When can you do it?

Garage   I'll book it in for tomorrow, brakes are a priority job. Actually, I've just looked at your service record, you're due for an interim service in three weeks. Would you like us to do that while the car is in? It would save you coming back again later.

Customer   That's a good idea, let's do that. I'll drop the car in first thing in the morning.

Garage   Don't worry about that. If you're worried about the brakes, I'll arrange for one of our mechanics to collect the car and return it in the evening. Actually, tomorrow we've got a courtesy car available, the mechanic can drop it off when he collects your car. We'll be round about 8.30 tomorrow if that's convenient.

If we look at that scenario again, here are the key processes.

- *Ask the customer for a unique identifier – name, registration / serial number, customer number.*

- *If possible, put the caller through to a named receptionist who has dealt with the customer before.*

- *Make sure the receptionist has access to full service information, ideally on computer.*

- *Take the opportunity to offer other services while the customer is having work carried out.*

- *Make it as convenient as possible for the customer to have work carried out.*

Organising your customer records

If you are running a small business with just a few important customers, there's a good chance that the people who take the calls will be familiar with customer details. But the larger the business, the less likely that is to happen. It's important that staff who take service calls have all the information to hand. These are the basics:

- *name and address of the customer;*
- *customer's product details;*
- *how long the customer has owned the product;*
- *service record, showing full history and recent details;*
- *information on any scheduled service requirements;*
- *notes about any faults or service problems incurred by the customer.*

By having that information to hand, you can avoid asking for details that the customer may resent giving you every time. It not only saves time on the phone, it looks more professional and it makes the customer feel that you value his business.

Next look for opportunities to make the most of the customer visit.

- *Include a prompt about any service jobs that could be brought forward to the current service.*
- *Make a note of any current service offers that you could offer the customer.*

Ideally, the information would be available on a personal computer, but paper-based systems can work equally effectively, provided they are easy to keep up-to-date.

Customer reception out of hours

You can introduce the most sophisticated call-handling systems or set up computerised records that provide all the information you need to handle incoming calls efficiently, but what happens if the customer has a problem and there is no-one there to deal with the request? Here are a number of tips to ensure that customers can always reach someone when they need help.

118

Provide 24-hour response

Customers usually have problems at the most inconvenient times. They may not need service immediately, but they feel more comfortable when they have reported a problem, discussed it with someone who knows what they are talking about and received reassurance that help will be on its way as quickly as possible. Out of hours, the service receptionist is likely to take details of the incident and make arrangements for all but the most urgent repairs the next working day. There are a number of ways in which 24-hour cover can be provided:

- setting up a shift system so that telephones are manned continuously;
- asking key personnel to take it in turns to handle emergency calls overnight; a call diversion system can be used to route calls to their home number;
- provide customers with mobile phone or home phone numbers of key personnel;
- appoint an agency to provide an out of hours call reception service.

119

Use 'postal reception'

This technique is used by car service companies or by companies that service small products. Typically a customer would have to wait till opening time just to hand over the keys or a product for repair. The customer may be late for work or suffer other inconvenience. With 'postal reception' he simply leaves the keys or the product in a secure area, such as a compound or mail box. This means that the customer can leave the product whenever it is most convenient.

Offer 'call back' facilities

The customer may not be able to reach you during working hours or may want to talk to someone but cannot get through because the contact is busy. By setting up a telephone answering or fax facility, you can make it easy for your customers to leave a request for a 'call back'. Provided you reply promptly, customers will appreciate the high level of service and they will save money on their own phone calls.

Summary

Customer reception is too important to be left to chance. You need to ensure that calls are answered promptly and efficiently and that the people answering the calls have all the information they need to deal with the caller in a professional manner. Telephone and computer technology can be used to improve performance in this area. You can also improve customer convenience by offering 'out of hours' reception to reassure the customer that help will be on the way.

16

Making every contact count

After the initial enquiries, how do you ensure that customers get the right treatment every time they deal with your company? This chapter looks at the importance of making every contact with the customer count by backing the staff who will deliver the highest standards of service to the customer and build effective long-term relationships.

Who does the customer contact

Customer focus depends on a consistently high standard of customer service over a long period of time, and that means building and maintaining a commitment to quality. Whenever a customer comes in contact with your organisation, they will be making a judgement about the quality of service they receive.

Depending on the size of the organisation, the people coming into contact with customers might include all staff or it may be a customer service team, representing the departments or functions that impinge directly on the customer. In a large manufacturing organisation, for example, the team might include people from the following departments:

- sales;
- distribution;
- manufacturing;
- design/development;

- personnel;
- training;
- purchasing;
- customer service;

- marketing;
- communications;

- quality;
- administration.

Selection factors

There are a number of factors which can be used to assess who should be included in the 'main team'.

- Their performance directly impinges on customer satisfaction;
- They are responsible for managing change which will influence the direction of customer service;
- They will be working closely with customers;
- They will be providing services which support customers.

The 'main team' will be working to achieve customer focus objectives and will be able to draw on the skills of other 'outer team' members to provide specialist support. Some examples show how this might work in practice.

Components supplier

An increasing number of components suppliers work in partnership with their customers to provide important business benefits, including guaranteed levels of quality supply, and to offer the manufacturer access to specialist technology. The partnership team might include:

- the general manager, responsible for the overall direction and quality of the partnership, plus high level relationships;
- the sales and marketing manager, responsible for commercial policies and service development;
- the production manager, responsible for maintaining the overall quality of supply;

- the quality manager, responsible for specific quality initiatives to meet the requirements of the partnership;
- the account manager or sales representative responsible for managing the day-to-day relationships between the supplier and the partners;
- the administration manager, responsible for developing communications and systems to support partnership;
- the research and development manager, responsible for developing new products to meet partners' requirements;
- the technical director, responsible for providing technical support to partners and managing technical relationships between the parties.

Capital equipment manufacturer

123

Capital equipment manufacturers provide their customers with a high level of technical co-operation and support to ensure that the customer is able to able to get an effective return on the investment, and obtain a high level of business benefits in the shortest possible time. Introducing the new equipment means considerable organisational change and skills development, so the initial emphasis within the customer team will be on customer support through the implementation period.

The team will include staff who can help the customer to manage the process of change, but the emphasis will be on customer support throughout the implementation period.

The team might include:

- the general manager to ensure effective high level relationships;
- the sales and marketing manager, responsible for the detailed commercial negotiations;
- the customer service manager, responsible for developing the right support programme to ensure effective implementation;

- the training manager, to help the customer develop the skills to take advantage of the new products;

- project managers, responsible for implementing the new system;

- the technical support manager, responsible for providing on-going advice and support to the customer's team during the start-up period.

Professional consultancy

A professional consultancy such as a marketing services company is delivering a service which supports customers' business objectives and the team will be focused on the delivery of the service. In a small consultancy, personal service is very important and the team will include those people who are directly involved with the partner's business. The team might include:

- the senior partner responsible for the overall direction of the business;

- the principal marketing consultant, responsible for the quality of the service;

- the marketing consultants who handle clients' business on a day-to-day basis;

- specialist consultants in disciplines such as research and communications.

Service organisation

A company that provides services such as repair and maintenance needs to build a team that combines the right skills with an infrastructure that makes it easy for the customer to do business. The team might include:

- the general manager responsible for the overall direction of the business;

- the operations manager responsible for developing an infrastructure that meets the partner's business requirements;

- the service manager, responsible for the delivery of service;
- the service development manager, responsible for introducing new services;
- senior managers responsible for specific service activities;
- branch managers responsible for the quality of local service delivery;
- service receptionists who deal with customers with service queries;
- service technicians who deliver the service;
- support staff who provide back-up services to the technicians.

Helping the team make effective contact

Earlier chapters of the book look at the specific skills required by different groups and individuals. However, to ensure the quality of day-to-day contact, it is important that every member of the team is committed to the following standards.

- *Deal with every customer courteously.*
- *Handle any enquiries promptly and efficiently.*
- *Agree to respond within set timescales.*
- *Keep other members of the team informed.*
- *Update members of the team on any problems or delays.*
- *Keep the customer informed at all times on the progress of enquiries and orders.*

It is easy to lose that vital direct contact when a team is dealing with the customer. Each member of the team assumes that someone else is taking responsibility for communication with the customer.

17

Build customer loyalty

Customers who stay with a company can provide long-term stability. It costs less to retain existing customers than to win new ones, and existing customers can be a valuable source of new business opportunities.

One of the key objectives of a customer service programme is therefore to retain customers over the long term – customers for life, even. Customers who are satisfied with the level and quality of service they receive are likely to continue buying from the same company. This degree of loyalty can be reinforced by customer retention programmes which reward customers for their loyalty in a way that further enhances customer service.

Follow up sales quickly

When a customer leaves the showroom, how quickly does the impact of the new product wear off? What happens if the customer discovers a problem? How can you reinforce the customer's loyalty from day one?

Make a courtesy call

A few days after customers have taken delivery of the product, call up to ask them how they found the product: are they still pleased with their choice, does it do what they expect, do they need any help in using the product, are there any unexpected problems? The same approach can be use after a service or repair. Is the fault cured or the product performing better? Was the customer completely satisfied with the way the service was carried out?

Send a letter

Sometimes a letter may have more impact than a phone call, particularly if it is a personal letter from someone senior in the company. The letter would cover the same points as the phone call and would invite the customer to call the senior manager personally if there were any concerns. Although this approach is less personal than a phone call, customers may feel it is less obtrusive. A letter also gives the customer time to think about a reply, and this may be more acceptable.

Send a questionnaire

You can ask the customer even more about the purchase and the product by sending a questionnaire. How do they find the product, were they pleased with the service they got, do they wish to make any comments about the service? A questionnaire is the least personal of the three approaches and you may not get a very high response, but the information can be valuable in identifying possible weaknesses in the sales process. On the opposite page is an example of a questionnaire from a retail outlet to customers who have bought consumer durable products.

Send the customer details of accessories or service

It's never too soon to start selling to the new customer. The offer of accessories that will enhance the original purchase or service to keep the product in top condition can help to reinforce the value of the original sale. On page 130 is an example of a letter from a local car dealer, inviting recent car buyers to join the Gold Card Club.

Customer Service
Questionnaire

Thank you for sparing a few minutes to fill in our customer service questionnaire. Your responses are of great value to us in identifying areas where we can improve our service to you. When you have completed the form, please return it in the stamped addressed envelope provided.

1 While you were in the showroom did a member
   of staff acknowledge you?   YES/NO

2 Did the salesperson introduce him or herself?   YES/NO

3 Which of the following questions did the
   salesperson ask?

   Style/range required   YES/NO

   Budget   YES/NO

   Accessories required   YES/NO

4 Did the salesperson provide any of the following?

   Brochure   YES/NO

   Details of the guarantee   YES/NO

   Price   YES/NO

   Business card   YES/NO

5 How satisfied were you with the sales/service you received?
   Delete as applicable:
   Very satisfied
   Fairly satisfied
   Not satisfied

If you would like to make any further comments please use the space below.

_____

_____

_____

129

Welcome to the Gold Card Club

∎

We are delighted that you have chosen to buy ... and we hope you enjoy many years of enjoyable, trouble-free motoring.

∎

To help you make the most of your new car, we would like to welcome you to the Gold Card Club.

∎

When you join, you will receive a free membership card which entitles you to a great range of savings and benefits.

∎

10 per cent discount and Courtesy Cars

For a start, you can get 10 per cent off all service, repair and parts bills. When you book a scheduled service in advance, you'll be entitled to a Courtesy Car.

∎

£100 worth of free accessories

As a special introductory bonus, we are pleased to offer you £100 worth of free accessories. You can take advantage of this offer for up to three months after you buy your car. Ask for our accessories catalogue now and make your choice.

∎

Keeping you in contact

The offers don't stop there. As a privileged member, you'll receive regular news about special membership offers and we'll keep you up-to-date with developments at our garage.

∎

Call to enrol now

Membership is free if you have bought a new or used car within the last four months. All you have to do is phone ... and give us your name and date of purchase. We'll send you your free Gold Card Club details.

∎

P.S. Don't forget to ask for an accessories catalogue and start choosing your £100 worth of free accessories.

Retaining customers

Activities like the Gold Card Club are just the beginning of a programme to retain customers. Contacting the customer just after the purchase is vital, but it is equally important to maintain contact six months, a year or several years after the original purchase.

Customer retention programmes can take many different forms, from simple concepts like discounts on repeat purchases, incentives for multiple purchases, to more complex frequent user programmes which provide rewards for customers who continue to use a service.

This chapter looks at different types of incentive schemes available and shows how a frequent user programme can be put into operation. Retention programmes are not just a form of sales incentive, they demonstrate that your organisation cares about its customers and is prepared to reward loyalty.

When loyalty programmes are important

Retention programmes are important in the following scenarios.

- Customers use the service frequently and the market is competitive.
- The loyalty programme proves to be an important differentiator.
- The retention programme provides an incentive to high levels of repeat purchase. Customers may use the product or service more frequently to gain additional points or prizes in the incentive programme.
- The incentive or reward itself provides an opportunity to demonstrate high levels of customer service. A frequent hotel user programme for example gives the customer an assured reservation, fast reception and a range of information to help make the traveller's life easier. Frequent flyer

clubs not only give customers points towards free travel, they also include free use of an executive lounge, simplified booking and check-in procedures. This in itself can increase customer satisfaction.

- The company is competing with other suppliers who offer similar services but do not have a customer service policy;

Frequent buyer programmes

Frequent buyer programmes that also accumulate information on customers are a powerful combination that strengthen the impact of customer focus programmes. An example is the frequent flyer programmes run by most of the major airlines. These provide regular travellers with points for every mile they fly which can be exchanged for free leisure travel. The British Airways programme has added an Executive Club which offers structured rewards to different groups of customers, according to their overall use of airline services. The scheme includes access to preferential seating, arrangements with hotels and car hire companies and access to executive airport lounges.

Retailer Argos operates a programme called Premier Points which issues points to customers for every ten pence they spend. The points are accumulated via a smart card, and the customer can use the points to pay for other purchases. Smart card technology is also increasingly used by petrol retailers as a tie in to their collector schemes. Instead of collecting vouchers or tokens, points are accumulated via the card. Multiple food retailers are also beginning to use a similar scheme to reward high spending customers.

Enhancing frequent buyer programmes

Frequent buyer programmes can be used to build a more complete picture of customers as a basis for detailed customer focus.

132

A smart card can provide detailed knowledge on purchasing patterns that provides a basis for cross-selling other products and services or tailoring products and services to the customer.

Summary

Customer loyalty programmes provide a basis for demonstrating high levels of customer care and differentiating the level of service. It is important that the reward reflects the company's customer service values and increases customer satisfaction. Although incentive programmes are used as part of a sales promotion programme, they also have a strategic role in building effective customer relationships. The most effective customer loyalty programmes not only reward regular customers, they provide information on their purchasing patterns as a basis for future product and service development.

133

18

Concentrate on aftersales service

Aftersales services can help you improve relationships with your customers and increase business. Look at your customers' buying cycle. How frequently do they make major purchases – monthly, annually, every three years, every five years? The longer the product cycle, the more difficult it is to maintain effective contact. Other companies can be talking to your customers, users may be experiencing problems that you are not aware of, and the decision-making team may be changing in ways that you cannot influence. Loss of contact could mean loss of control.

In the consumer sector, car manufacturers realised that the period between new car sales is the most critical element of customer relations. With customers buying new cars every two to three years on average, sales control is minimal. Manufacturers have therefore focused their efforts on building an effective aftersales operation based on the fact that parts and service operations generate five times the number of customer contacts as new car sales. The manufacturers realised that they had been losing both repair and scheduled maintenance work to 'fast-fit' operations. This meant a loss of revenue to their dealerships, but also denied them the opportunity to maintain customer satisfaction between car purchases.

The same principle can be applied to the information technology market where new system sales have similar purchase lead times of several years. Computer manufacturers had been losing maintenance business to independent service companies; they also found that the customers' information systems strategy and choice of systems was being driven, not by the manu-facturers, but by management consultancies. When manage-ment consultancies moved into other areas of information systems service such as application development and managed service, and when independent service companies expanded their activities, the computer manufacturers lost even more account control.

Although service companies and management consultancies were not the manufacturers' direct competitors, they were enjoying high levels of contact with key decision-makers at senior and middle management level, and this influenced future business opportunities. By introducing a broad range of cus-tomer services, the manufacturers would be able to build high levels of contact with decision-makers throughout the customer organisation.

136

Improving loyalty and contact

As the previous section mentioned, customer contact is one of the most important benefits of a customer service programme. If we take the example of the computer manufacturer, we can iden-tify a number of stages where customer service can be used to increase the frequency and quality of customer contact:

- **Strategic consultancy** – helping the customer develop an information systems strategy in line with corporate objec-tives. This brings the company into contact with the senior executive team and provides valuable information on the customer's future business plans.

- **Information systems consultancy** – turning the strat-egy into a practical solution. This provides contact opportu-nities at senior executive and operational levels.

- **Implementation services** – helping the customer to install and introduce a new system without recruiting spe-cialist staff or overloading his own support staff. This helps to ensure that the customer's system is implemented effectively, increasing customer satisfaction and loyalty.

- **Training services** – providing the customer with skills development and building useful contact with departmental managers and users.

- **Managed services** – which cover a wide range of maintenance and systems management activities. This provides the supplier with one of the best opportunities for continuous contact with information systems staff and gives the supplier a valuable insight into the customer's changing systems needs.

There are many other services that could be included on this list, but they demonstrate the principle of improved contact. These services also make an important contribution to the success of a customer's business and that, in turn, can improve customer loyalty. If a customer was to provide those services internally, it would put considerable pressure on his own resources or prevent him achieving the full benefits of his investment in the new system. Customers therefore become dependent on your services for the efficient running of their own operations, and this can help to strengthen relationships.

137

Identifying service opportunities

One of the most effective ways to identify service opportunities is to look at the problems your customers face by analysing a series of business scenarios. Some examples show how the process works.

- *Your customers need to ensure that they have devised the right strategy to meet their business objectives.* They need objective advice and guidance to improve the quality of their own decision-making. You could meet those requirements by offering consultancy services.

- *Your customers have identified certain activities which are crucial to their business success.* They need help in defining the problems and planning the most appropriate course of action. Consultancy will also be relevant here.

■ *Your customers need to adapt quickly to changing market conditions or competitive threats,* but they do not have the resources or skills to succeed. You can offer your customers your skills and resources on a project basis so that they can overcome short- and long-term requirements.

■ *Your customers need to develop new user and management skills* so that they can get the best return from the products and services they have bought from you. You can offer your customers training services.

■ *Your customers need to ensure that their products are continually operational* and providing the business benefits they were designed for. By offering your customers maintenance services or managing their equipment for them, you can ensure that their products are kept in the best possible condition.

Technical support

Technical support is one of the most common types of customer service and it can take many forms:

■ technical advisory service;

■ design and application service;

■ field technical support;

■ installation.

Technical support is vital if your company is supplying components or technical products and services. Your technical support can help your customers to improve the performance of their products and make them more competitive in their own markets. By working closely with the customer design team, you can ensure that your company becomes a preferred supplier for new products. Involvement in the product development phase enables your team to get a better feel for your customers' product plans and technical problems that you can overcome.

A high level of technical service is essential if your company supplies complex products or services or if your customers are developing new products, but technical service can also help to differentiate commodity products and basic components.

A bearing manufacturer supplying transmission bearings worked closely with an equipment manufacturer to rationalise the design of a new product through value engineering. By substituting a transmission bearing with integral housing, sealing and lubrication facility for a series of separate components, the manufacturer was able to reduce machining and assembly costs. The bearing supplier was able to put considerable distance between his added-value engineering solution and a standard component, and overcome price comparisons. The company was also able to build closer working relationships with the design department and to build future modifications and product developments into the customer's forward plans.

139

Project management

Project management services help customers to take on or complete projects for which they do not have the skills or resources. By using your skilled staff, they can have the project carried out by experienced specialists and they do not have to recruit new staff or retrain their own. Projects can be long-term or short-term and might include:

- installing new products or systems;
- helping to redesign a product;
- carrying out specialist services or maintenance work;
- introducing a new departmental or corporate operating procedure.

The customer may need support because his own staff are

overloaded or because he wants them to concentrate on core business activities. To encourage customers to use your project services, you may need to explain the hidden cost benefits of using outside specialists:

- The customer can respond to threats or opportunities quickly.

- The customer can introduce new business processes quickly without disrupting day-to-day activities.

- Projects will be carried out to the highest standards by specialists.

- Projects will be completed within an agreed timescale without recruiting staff or diverting internal staff.

- Projects will be handled cost-effectively compared with internal resources.

140

Management consultancies use project services to implement their strategic recommendations and retain control over the account. They are aware that customers may not understand the full management implications of fundamental changes and, therefore, may fail to achieve the full business benefit. If the management team feel disappointed with the results, they may blame the consultancy. It is important to the consultancy's long-term business prospects that their recommendations are properly implemented so project services play a vital role.

Training services

Training services help your customers make the most effective use of the products they buy from you, or provide them with additional skills to improve their business performance. In the computer industry, for example, training is offered at a number of different levels.

- **Senior executive courses in planning and managing information systems.** The training programmes help executives relate their information systems to their corporate objectives and ensure that they select the correct system. This type of training helps improve the quality of decision-making and demonstrates that the supplier is helping the customer to improve business performance.

- **Courses for departmental managers in using information systems.** The training programmes help departmental managers understand how information systems will impinge on their day-to-day operations and provides them with guidelines on managing their systems. This type of training builds understanding and overcomes any potential resistance in the decision-making team.

- **Courses for information systems specialists.** This type of training improves specialists' skills and keeps them up-to-date with the suppliers' latest technical developments.

- **Courses for operators and users.** This is the traditional type of training included in a product/service package. It is an essential element, ensuring that the product is used correctly.

141

- **Courses for systems support staff.** This type of training helps reduce the service load on the supplier. By ensuring that customers' internal support staff can deal with day-to-day queries and system management, the supplier can use his support specialists to deliver higher-value services.

The training can be delivered in a number of ways:

- using an internal training department and employing training specialists at a central site;

- delivering training services at the customer's site using your own training specialists;

- using an independent training organisation to deliver training;

- developing distance learning packages or publishing training material for use by the customer's own training specialists.

Training services add value to the account relationship by

improving the customer's overall business performance. They should be an integral part of your aftersales programme if the following conditions apply.

- Your products are technically complex.
- The introduction of your product will bring about fundamental change in the customer's organisation.
- Your customers do not have the product experience to make effective purchasing decisions.
- Your technology changes rapidly.

Maintenance and facilities management services

142

Although few companies would overlook product maintenance as an integral element of their product/service package, the method of delivering maintenance can improve account control.

- To overcome the threats from independent maintenance companies, suppliers are developing more sophisticated, quality-controlled maintenance services. They invest in service tools specially tailored to their products or set up service databases which enable rapid fault diagnosis or preventative maintenance.
- Suppliers offer their customers different levels of service, for example gold, silver or bronze standard. These options which include differences in level of cover, response time, spares holding and cost can be fine-tuned to provide customers with a tailored service that matches their support requirements.
- Managed service, where a supplier takes over complete responsibility for managing all service activities on site equipment, is a valuable approach when customers have bought equipment from a number of different suppliers and have to co-ordinate different service suppliers. The managed service provider liaises with the other manufacturers' service

departments, co-ordinates their activities, imposes quality standards and provides the customer with a single invoice. The customer benefits from more consistent standards of service and simpler administration, while the supplier increases account control and reduces competitive threats.

- Facilities management where a supplier takes over the complete management and maintenance of a customer's equipment is more appropriate than managed service where the customer's equipment is predominantly supplied by one manufacturer. As part of the facilities management contract, the manufacturer upgrades the equipment so that it always reflects the latest product development. The customer does not have to provide any support staff, so is free to concentrate on core business activities.

This type of service is a long way from the 'fix it when it goes wrong' approach, and it demonstrates how maintenance can deliver powerful customer benefits. It not only ensures that the customer's equipment is kept in the best condition, it can reduce the burden of service administration and free service staff for more productive tasks.

143

Selling services

Services can be a major contributor to account control and may increase revenue and profit. However, there are a number of obstacles to overcome in selling services.

- You may have supplied certain services free of charge as part of an overall package. You now need to persuade your customers that they should pay for those services. You need to explain how chargeable services add value and help the customer improve business performance.

- Your customers may not realise that they need certain services. You have to explain the business benefits and the hidden cost benefits of support services. Relating your services to the customer's business scenarios improves understanding.

■ Your salesforce may be reluctant to sell services because they are low in value compared with capital products. You must stress the account control benefits of service support and encourage the salesforce to invest time for long-term benefit.

Summary

Services make a major contribution to quality customer service by increasing the frequency of contact between product purchase and helping your customers improve their business performance. Customers need different forms of support depending on whether they are introducing a new product or trying to get the maximum business benefit from using it.

144

19

Use complaints in a positive way

The value of complaints

Customers who have their complaints resolved are likely to remain loyal customers, and tell friends and colleagues how their complaints have been handled. But what happens to the rest, do they complain with their feet, do they remain silently resentful or do they tell their friends about the bad service they have endured?

Complaints are vital to a customer-focused company. They highlight weaknesses in customer service, identify areas for improvement and provide an opportunity to demonstrate high levels of customer care.

Encouraging complaints

How can you make the most of complaints?

- *Encourage customers to complain – put up signs, provide addresses or phone numbers on all customer communications.*
- *Make it easy for customers to complain by providing a free-phone number or freepost address and giving customers a named contact.*
- *Make sure that the nominated phone line is manned by someone experienced in customer-handling skills.*
- *Give the contact the authority to resolve complaints and, if necessary to provide reasonable compensation.*

- *Ensure that an escalation process is in position to deal with complaints that cannot be resolved immediately.*
- *Thank the customer for highlighting the problem and allowing the company to resolve it.*
- *Assure customers that remedial action will be taken.*
- *Set up a process for recording and analysing complaints.*

A positive attitude to complaints can bring its rewards. The financial performance of Marks & Spencer, for example, has not suffered as a result of their commitment to settling complaints without fuss.

Analysing the cause of customer complaints

146

There is often a clear difference between the expression of customer dissatisfaction and its cause.

Consider a customer who experiences a series of relatively minor problems with his bank. An automatic payment has been missed, the cheque book is not available at the branch as requested, the application for a new credit card has been delayed by a week. While each of these has been fixed by the bank, the customer has just experienced a series of unsatisfactory events.

Finally, the customer visits a branch, joining a long queue. When she reaches the counter, she is told that she will need to go to another counter to have that matter attended to. The customer explodes in an 'irrational' outburst of dissatisfaction. She immediately blames branch staff, claiming they are either unwilling or unable to attend to their request. The outburst is out of all proportion to the difficulty being experienced.

The customer is, however, expressing dissatisfaction with a poor relationship at the only point where that dissatisfaction can be heard by someone representing the company the front line staff. Yet, in reality, it is not the behaviour of the front line staff which has caused dissatisfaction, but on-going problems with the end-to-end relationship.

A customer-focused organisation will spend time analysing their customer information to identify the causes of customer complaints. After analysing the likely cause of customer comments, the organisation will need to determine its response to any situation. A customer-focused organisation is one which always looks to internal changes to alleviate, remedy or improve the experience of the customer in dealing with it.

Making it easy to complain

An attempt to make a complaint to a national electrical retailer resulted in four phone calls, and no satisfactory outcome. The first call to head office was answered by a receptionist who didn't understand the meaning of the term 'customer service'. The customer was referred to the national service centre in another location. The national service centre told the caller its role was to co-ordinate service requests and suggested the caller try the appropriate regional office. The regional office assumed the caller had a problem with the product and asked for details of the purchase. When the caller explained that the complaint was not about the product, but about the company, he was told to 'write to head office'. The customer was not impressed.

147

In another example, a customer wanted to return a rented portable television set that was no longer required to a national rental company. The local branch arranged for collection and amended the customer's account. Two days after making the arrangements, the customer received a call from the company's customer service department to ask whether everything was all right, and to check that the customer was not returning the set because of a problem or a complaint. The company had taken the initiative and anticipated a potential problem. This customer was impressed by the proactive service. If there had been a problem, it is likely that it would have been resolved.

Here are some ways in which you can encourage customers to complain and demonstrate a caring attitude.

- *Include a telephone number or address in all communications material and preferably make it free.*
- *Make sure that all customer-facing staff are aware of the procedures for complaining.*
- *If necessary, produce a guide on 'how to complain' which lays out the options open to the customer.*
- *In a retail outlet, provide a clearly marked area for customer service.*
- *Where possible, anticipate potential complaints by following up any 'returns'.*

Responding to complaints

148

Customers expect a prompt and positive response to their complaints. Whether you telephone or write depends on the nature and timing of the problem, but you should take the opportunity not only to deal with the problem, but reassure the customer that you are committed to the highest standards of service. Here are four examples of a letter from a service company dealing with a customer who, up to this point, has had a poor response from the company.

Version 1   Problem now solved

Thank you for letting us know that you are now fully satisfied with . . . . While we aim to achieve the highest standards from the outset, we understand that problems can occur and we are pleased that you took the trouble to bring it to our attention.

We aim to respond positively to our customers' concerns and we will be looking very closely at the particular . . . . process that was used. We hope that you would wish to use our services on future occasions and we look forward to dealing with you.

Thank you once again for contacting . . . .

Version 2   Company unable to contact customer

You recently contacted us about . . . . problem. I wanted to discuss this with you personally over the telephone, but I have been unable to reach you. If you would like to contact . . . . (name/number of someone who can take calls for you) and let them know when we can reach you, I will call you back.

I am sorry to hear that you have a problem and I would like to settle the matter as quickly as possible. While we aim to achieve the highest standards from the outset, we understand that problems can occur and we are pleased that you took the trouble to bring it to our attention. We aim to respond positively to our customers' concerns and we will be looking very closely at the particular . . . . process that was used.

Thank you once again for contacting . . . . and I hope to speak to you very soon.

149

Version 3   Problem doing the rounds

You recently contacted . . . . about . . . . problem and I understand that you have not yet had a satisfactory reply. I am sorry that there has been a delay and I am now taking personal responsibility for the matter.

Either

I wanted to discuss this with you personally over the telephone, but I have been unable to reach you. If you would like to contact . . . . . . (name/number of someone who can take calls for you) and let them know when we can reach you, I will call you back.

or

I want to discuss this with you personally over the telephone, and I will be contacting you in the next few days.

I hope that we can then settle the matter as quickly as possible. While we aim to achieve the highest standards from the outset, we understand that problems can occur and we are pleased that you took the trouble to bring it to our attention. We aim to respond positively to our customers' concerns and we will be looking very closely at the particular . . . . process that was used.

Thank you once again for contacting . . . . and I hope to speak to you very soon.

Version 4 Problem needs specialist reply

> You recently contacted . . . . about . . . . problem and I understand that you have not yet had a satisfactory reply. I am sorry that there has been a delay and I am now taking personal responsibility for the matter.
>
> Your query is being investigated by a specialist in . . . . department and I have asked that person to report back to me within . . . . . days. I will then telephone you to discuss the matter and, if necessary, arrange for the specialist to contact you directly.
>
> I hope that we can then settle the matter as quickly as possible. While we aim to achieve the highest standards from the outset, we understand that problems can occur and we are pleased that you took the trouble to bring it to our attention. We aim to respond positively to our customers' concerns and we will be looking very closely at the particular . . . . process that was used.
>
> Thank you once again for contacting . . . . and I hope to speak to you very soon.

150

Awkward complaints

Those letters cover situations where the customer is right, and the company has been at fault in handling the complaint. However, the situation could be more complicated and sometimes the customer may have a complaint that is not entirely justified. By anticipating problems and developing a suitable response, you will be able to handle customer complaints more effectively.

Here is a series of scenarios that you might face:

- problem with the product;
- poor service quality;
- product no longer available;
- parts delayed;
- product out of guarantee;

- late delivery of product;
- demand for compensation for poor service;
- customer has damaged product;
- product incapable of repair;
- offer of alternative;
- customer wants to make a formal complaint;
- customer/company cannot settle a dispute.

Each of those scenarios can put a company in a difficult situation if it is not prepared.

Learning from complaints

Although an effective complaints-handling procedure is vital, it is also essential to use complaints as a form of research that enables you to improve products and business processes. To make the most of customer complaints, set up a process for recording, analysing and taking action.

151

- *Ensure that all complaints are recorded.*
- *Identify the source of the complaint and assess whether corrective action is needed.*
- *Monitor the frequency of different types of complaint to set priorities for action programmes.*
- *Monitor product and process performance after corrective action has been taken.*

Summary

Complaints can be used in a positive way to demonstrate high levels of customer care and identify problems within an organisation. By responding positively and utilising this form of research you can improve products and business processes so that they meet customer needs more effectively.

20

Maintaining relationships

Building and maintaining effective customer relationships is one of the most crucial challenges facing any company, and success can only be judged in the eyes of customers.

Here's how one financial institution identified that successful customer relationships were crucial to its future success. It carried out a customer satisfaction survey and these were the key findings:

- Customer satisfaction improved from 65 per cent to 69 per cent nationally
- 7/8 of the top 10 customer issues are relationship-related
- Customers like relationships to be in place for a reasonable length of time

The results also showed improvements in the top three relationship issues:

Supportiveness	+ 3%
Understanding	+ 3%
Speed of decision	+ 4%

Those are the issues that customers feel are important and those are the areas where customer service programmes could be used to strengthen the position even further.

The survey also show how customers' perceptions of the importance of different factors are changing. Overall, the results confirm that the quality of relationships remain top of the agenda from the customer's point of view, while charges have fallen from top spot to third. Listed in the table are the top ten customer issues and you can see how important relationships are:

1994		1993
1	Being supportive of my business	2
2	Understanding my business	3
3	Current account transaction charges	1
4	Speed of decisions (on lending)	5
5	Credibility and authority of main account contact	6
6	Continuity of main account contact	7
7	Autonomy of account contact in decisions that affect my business	8
8	Accessibility of main account contact	9
9	Speed of carrying out instructions	12
10	Reliable and efficient service in the branch	10

The survey gives a valuable insight into the type and quality of service customers want from the organisation. It also helps to highlight where it is strong and where it needs to improve its performance.

What customers said about the service

These were some of the important comments from customers that help to highlight the type of relationship they want with the organisation.

Customers want to deal with people who understand their business.

'We appreciate the trouble taken to understand our business which has to cope with particularly severe seasonality.'
'A manager who's in touch with today's business needs.'

Customers want their bank to be supportive and approachable.

'Feeling that the door is always open.'
'Very approachable, easy to discuss ideas and problems with.'

Customers expect professional, efficient service.

'A very friendly and efficient bank, it's always a pleasure to visit.'
'The relationship strength between the bank and our business is entirely down to the efficiency, accuracy and helpfulness of the Business Banker who offers a quality personal service.'

Continuity is as vital as service quality

'In my experience, there is little that frightens businesses more than the news that their Bank Manager is about to change. The challenge is to improve the way we handle that change.' – The director of a major UK bank

155

Although the organisation identified that it had made good progress in relationship issues, it realised that continuity of relationships was important to customers. In both the Questionnaire and the Customer Satisfaction Index, customers expressed concern about the impact of personnel changes on their business relationships.

Customers feel that continuity is important and, although an organisation may not be able to avoid change, it can minimise risk by handling the change professionally and efficiently in a structured but customer-friendly way.

There are a number of important considerations in managing a handover.

- Time and effort should be prioritised in managing relationships with the most important customers.
- There is a threat that the customer may defect because of the strength of the existing relationship.

- The company should emphasise continuity not change in communications with customers.
- Incoming and outgoing staff should share customer information to ensure that a full understanding is built up.
- The incoming people should take an early opportunity to demonstrate an understanding of the customer's business.

Ten ways to improve relationships

Here are some tips that could help you improve relationships with your customers.

Remember

1 **Be friendly** – others will respond.
2 **Be honest and open** – it is the best policy.
3 **Be polite** – manners do not cost anything.
4 **Be interested in others** – they will be interested in you.
5 **Be cheerful** – whatever you are doing.
6 **Be tolerant** – everyone makes mistakes.
7 **Be sympathetic** – customers want support.
8 **Be fair** – it is all that is expected.
9 **Be tactful** – you are in a position of trust.
10 **Be positive** – 'can do' people achieve.

Building and maintaining effective customer relationships is one of the most crucial challenges facing any organisation. Those ten tips can help you focus on the quality of those relationships in day-to-day dealings with customers.

Regular communications

How do your customers perceive you? Do you keep them up to

date with all the developments in your organisation? Whenever you talk to customers, make presentations or plan more formal communications, you should seek to build a positive image.

These are some of the factors that help to build effective relationships and encourage a customer to have confidence in a supplier.

- The company is a professional organisation which understands the customer's business needs and can meet them with a wide range of high quality products and services.
  - The company is technically successful in major projects, developing total solutions and delivering value for money, on time, every time.
  - The company is winning share from its competitors.
  - The company is an approved and respected strategic supplier with whom it is safe to place business.
  - The company is a successful and financially stable company with a sound management team – a good prospective supplier and business partner.

157

Communicating professionalism

'The company is a professional organisation which understands the customer's business needs and can meet them with a wide range of high-quality products and services.' The messages to support this perception include:

- The company is investing £** in training over the next year.
- The company is organised into market-focused groups to offer the highest standards of service.
- *** staff are dedicated to the customer's business.
- The company is committed to total quality.
- The company has developed a broad product range and a full range of support services.
- The company's products meet international standards.
- The new product development programme is providing innovative new products.

Communicating technical success

'The company is technically successful in major projects, developing total solutions and delivering value for money, on time, every time.' The important messages to support this perception include:

- The company has an established reputation for innovation.
- The company's products have been selected for the following demanding applications . . . .
- Customers are saving money by using the company's products.
- The company's products conform to international standards.
- The company has a research and development budget in excess of £*** and has a team of *** highly skilled people dedicated to technical support.

Communicating market success

'The company is winning share from its competitors.' The important messages to support this perception include:

- The company has been selected to provide products and services to the following customers . . . .
- The company has recently won a major order worth £*****
- The company has been selected as a strategic supplier to the following customers . . . .
- The company has gained ** per cent market share in the last year, while competitors have lost ** per cent share in the last year.

Communicating strategic supplier status

'The company is an approved and respected strategic supplier with whom it is safe to place business.' The important messages to support this perception include:

- The company has been selected as a strategic supplier to the following market-leading customers . . . .
- The company is collaborating with a major international organisation.
- The company meets the following international product and quality standards . . . .

Communicating corporate stability

'The company is a successful and financially stable company with a sound management team – a good prospective supplier and business partner.' The important messages to support this perception include:

- The company's annual results show ** per cent growth in orders, revenue and profits.
- The company is expanding.
- The company is a member of the *** international group.
- The company is the leading European supplier.

159

Send your customers product updates

It is vital that your customers' technical and purchasing specialists always have the latest information on your products. This is not only sound engineering practice, it alerts them to any new developments that may help them to develop their own products. You can use a formal system of change control to ensure that each of your contacts is kept up-to-date.

Keep your customers up to date with technical and research developments

These are similar to product updates, but they notify your customers of future developments so that they can incorporate new technology into their own forward programmes. This type of update not only enhances your technical reputation, it helps to build closer working relationships between the technical groups. These updates can be published occasionally or at regular intervals, say quarterly or annually.

Run customer team briefings on corporate progress

Significant developments such as new investment programmes, acquisitions, changes in management, expansion programmes or new product launches are of major interest to your key account customers. By bringing together the two teams, you can take the opportunity to update everyone on progress and ensure that there are experts on hand to deal with specific issues.

160

Send your customers corporate/financial information

Although financial information is an integral element of the team briefing process, you can keep individual decision-makers up-to-date by sending copies of corporate brochures, financial results and other corporate information. A regular flow of information will ensure that key influencers are aware of your financial performance and remain confident of your ability as a stable supplier.

Tell your customers about the company direction

It is important that your key customers understand the future direction of your company – how do you see your business in the medium- and long-term, what new developments do you plan to introduce, and are you considering any fundamental changes to your business? They need to be convinced that you will remain committed to the success of their business and that they will continue to benefit from working closely with you. An understanding of your future direction helps your customers plan their own development.

Check that your customers are satisfied

As well as keeping customers informed of developments in your company, it is also important to monitor their attitudes to your company and your performance on their account. Customer satisfaction surveys are covered in more detail in Chapter 24, 'Monitor customer satisfaction levels', but they should be an integral element of a two-way communications strategy.

161

Hold customer performance review meetings

As well as measuring customer satisfaction, you should be prepared to review your performance with your key customers and discuss measures for improving performance. By taking a proactive attitude to performance measurement, you demonstrate high levels of customer care and improve relationships with team members. Review meetings can be held at a number of different levels:

- **monthly progress meetings** on technical and commercial matters, involving specialist members of the team;
- **quarterly review meetings** on overall performance – most of the team will participate and the meeting will be used to identify any remedial actions needed;
- **annual reviews** involving senior members of the team to review performance and discuss key objectives for the coming year.

Tell customers about your organisation

In a customer/supplier relationship where a large number of people are involved, an account team manual can be extremely useful. The manual should include all the information needed to operate the account, and would be distributed to members of both teams. The contents of the manual might include:

- introductory section on the general benefits of working together, focusing on the opportunities to improve business performance and maintain a competitive edge;
- the key performance measurements used to assess progress;
- the scope of the account relationship, including supply and distribution arrangements, action programmes and levels of technical and marketing co-operation;
- an outline of the direction in which the account could develop, including a growth path and possible action programmes;
- the quality processes and feedback mechanisms that would be used to control the programme;
- the skills and resources of both companies;
- the organisation of the two companies, including appropriate personnel details;
- the responsibilities of both parties and the reporting procedures;
- contact information explaining the communications links between the two companies and the sources of information within each;
- escalation procedures to deal with any problems on the account;
- a summary of the main benefits and long-term objectives of the account relationship.

The manual is a valuable technique for building understanding and maintaining relationships between the two parties. It ensures that everyone understands their role and shows how the relationship can be utilised to provide benefits for both parties.

Summary

Regular communication with customers at all levels is essential to maintaining effective customer relationships. Regular briefings on corporate, financial and technical developments build confidence and ensure that your company is regarded as a stable supplier. It is also important to assess customer attitudes to your performance and discuss improvement programmes through a series of regular team progress meetings. Large account teams can become unwieldy, but an account team manual will help to keep both parties informed about each other.   163

21

Offer customers a helpline

If you've been through the traumas of buying a personal computer, you'll understand the problems of trying to choose from hundreds of 'me too' products, each one claiming to offer the ultimate solution to your needs. If you then tried to work out which of the manufacturers' extensive hardware/software packages was right for you, you'll understand why customers sometimes need help in choosing a product.

The right advice before a sale can demonstrate customer service from the outset and win loyal customers. That's why increasing numbers of computer companies provide customers and prospects with a freephone helpline and encourage them to talk.

Here's how they make the most of the phone.

- The freephone facility encourages people to use the service and discuss their requirements at length.

- The helplines are manned by specialists who combine technical knowledge with an ability to talk to individuals at the right level – callers are not intimidated by talking to people who reply in jargon.

- Helpline staff talk about the customer's needs – how do you plan to use the computer, what results do you want, how often do you use it? They concentrate on identifying the customer's needs, not doing a sales pitch on their products.

- Staff are encouraged to develop a relationship over the phone, not deal with queries as quickly as possible and meet a daily target. Dialogue and a relaxed attitude help to build customer confidence.

The customer who gets honest, straightforward answers will trust the company. In a commodity market, that level of customer service can be an important differentiator.

So, don't just reserve helplines for operating problems or service requests. Use them to build a relationship before the selling starts. Once you have established customer needs, your sales team can concentrate on offering the right product. The result – customer satisfaction at every stage.

Use 'support' helplines to reduce inconvenience

166

When customers have a problem, it is reassuring that they can come straight through to a helpline to get help, advice, support and comfort. Here is an example (opposite) of a brochure from an accident repair company who offer customers who have had an accident a freephone helpline anywhere in the country.

Why customers welcome 'support' helplines

Customers who can relax knowing that their problems are taken care of will be fully satisfied with the services that are available and will be happy to deal with the same outlet in the future. Research into service standards indicated that reassurance was one of the prime considerations.

Psychologists working with quality experts found out that a key factor in delivering time-guaranteed services was the ability to reassure customers that help was on the way. Customers would then be prepared to wait until help or support arrived even if there was a long gap between reporting the incident and having it resolved. So, if vital manufacturing equipment broke down, the equipment supplier would offer a 24-hour, 4-hour or 1-hour call out service. Customers, as research showed, were not

We would like to welcome you as a member of Global Crash Repair Services. If you should be unfortunate enough to have an accident, you can rest assured that we will do everything to get you and your car back to normal as soon as possible. All you have to do is call one number free and you'll be in touch with experienced incident controllers who will take care of everything for you.

Our aim is to help you get to your next destination as smoothly and as quickly as possible, and to provide you with a high-quality repair service that gets your own car back on the road as quickly as possible. Driver care is our priority and you'll find the whole service simple and carefree. Here's what happens.

- Just dial the freephone number, wherever you are in the country.
- We bring a replacement car to you at the site of the accident.
- If you are unable to drive, we can arrange accommodation or transport to your destination.
- Your car will be taken to one of our own repair centres and returned to you when the work is complete.

167

In short, you can forget about the hassle of the accident and get on with the next stage of your journey. You won't have to track down the nearest recovery agent or repair centre, search for change for the phone or worry about meeting those unexpected bills. Best of all, you'll have a friendly voice just a phone call away if you need help or advice, or if you want to find out what's happening.

Accidents usually happen in the most inconvenient places and the last thing you want to do after an accident is co-ordinate a rescue and recovery service. Membership of Global Crash Repair Services means you can leave it all to the experts. One freephone number puts you in touch, wherever you are, and our incident controllers take care of everything. All you have to do is give your membership number and your location. Our local team will bring a replacement car to the site of the accident so you'll be mobile straight away. If you prefer public transport to your next destination or if you would rather stay overnight, we'll make all the arrangements on your behalf. You might need legal advice or other help after the accident, just ask when you call.

If you have any questions about Global Crash Repair Services, call freephone 0800 123456. Remember there's only one number to dial if you have an accident.

too concerned how long the repair would take provided they were kept informed.

The same principles can be applied to any service-led organisation where the customer needs to be kept informed – maintenance and support services on vital equipment, for example, or disaster recovery services where the customer faces many difficult and unfamiliar decisions, and needs constant support to reassure them. Companies who provide traveller's cheques offer their customers a 24-hour helpline anywhere in the world to get financial help or advice on their holiday money. Lost cheques or exchange problems can be handled efficiently with minimum disruption to the holiday, giving the customer peace of mind and increasing customer satisfaction.

Insurance companies offer their customers helplines for motoring cases or domestic problems. The customer can call, get immediate support services, plus advice on how to proceed and make a claim. The same principle of reassurance applies. During an incident, the customer can be uncertain of how to proceed, and welcomes advice and guidance to minimise distress and inconvenience.

When is a 'support' helpline important?

A number of scenarios can be used to identify situations where support like this could be valuable.

- The customer could suffer a great deal of inconvenience and stress as a result of the incident – reducing the stress and inconvenience would help to demonstrate high levels of care and increase customer satisfaction.
- The incident could threaten the efficiency of the company business and measures must be taken to limit the damage.
- The customer does not have the skills and resources to resolve the problems on the spot and is dependent on external forms of support.

- The customer has paid for a support package and has agreed to a certain level of response. The company must respond within the agreed levels;

- The speed of response is seen as a competitive differentiator and is positioned as an integral part of the service package.

- Failure to deal with the incident quickly could have a critical effect on the customer's business or personal activities.

- The incident could have legal implications and the customer needs high levels of advice and guidance.

What service should the 'support' helpline offer?

The helpline plays a vital part in building this reassurance and helping customers deal with problems with the minimum of inconvenience. This example from one of the motoring rescue organisations shows some of the key services a helpline can provide. It:

169

- takes the incoming call from the customer, establishes location and identifies the form of support needed;

- provides individual guidance to the customer on action to be taken with an indication of the support that will be provided;

- deals with the customers' immediate queries;

- makes detailed arrangements to put support services into operation, makes hotel, hire car or hotel bookings on behalf of the customer and arranges settlement;

- informs family or business colleagues on the customer's behalf;

- monitors progress on the support services and keeps the customer up-to-date if possible. Many telephone companies are now bundling vehicle rescue services with mobile phones to ensure that a customer can be kept up to date during an incident.

This support service compares favourably with all the problems customers might face if they had to co-ordinate all the support activities themselves – contacting a rescue organisation, finding a repair centre, booking a hotel, getting to the next destination or home by public transport while being in a state of distress after a breakdown or accident.

Using 'information' helplines

So far we have looked at ways in which customers can use helplines to discuss products before a sale, or get help if they have a problem. Helplines can also be useful to give customers up-to-date information. However, dealing with simple queries can tie up valuable staff time so it's worth thinking about using some of the low-cost answering or voicemail systems that are now available.

Recent research from the telecommunications industry suggests that around 76 per cent of calls are not completed at the first attempt. The extension is engaged, the contact is not there, or the caller got through to the wrong extension. It is frustrating for anyone who wants to make an enquiry, so how can you make it easier for customers to get information over the phone? One solution would be to appoint more people to answer the phone, but that could be expensive and may not be cost-effective.

Callers may not want dialogue

Consider some further research findings – 50 per cent of those calls were single-directional – the callers did not want to have a discussion, they just wanted to obtain or leave information. Is the solution to set up a central message centre? The research does little to encourage this approach. Of telephone messages taken by a third party, 90 per cent are believed to be inaccurate or incomplete in some way.

Give callers a choice

Voicemail is another possible solution. At its simplest, voicemail is the electronic equivalent of a personal mailbox. Callers can leave messages knowing that their contact will deal with them on their return. There is no problem in the accuracy of message handling and messages can be communicated to other people in the organisation.

Voicemail can also be used as the basis of a sophisticated customer response system. For example, by keying certain digits, the caller can access information services, request literature, leave a private message, get through to an operator or initiate other actions.

The technology to support voicemail is becoming more widely available and is no longer the preserve of the larger company.

171

Customer-focused response mechanisms

By providing these options, a company can develop a customer-focused response mechanism that demonstrates high levels of customer care and convenience. Among the possible options are:

- 24-hour ordering systems that do not require staff presence;
- a literature request service;
- a dial-up price or delivery information service.

Voicemail can be seen as an impersonal, machine-based system, but the customer service benefits are considerable.

Summary

Helplines can play an important part in improving service to customers. They can be used to talk customers through unfamiliar products, and build their confidence before a sale. They can also be used to provide support to customers who are experiencing problems. Information helplines can be used to provide customers with up-to-date information during the sales process. Technology is now widely available to help you run helplines without tying up valuable staff time.

22

Improve the efficiency of administration

Poor service at the checkout, late delivery, missing parts, inaccurate invoicing or other forms of administrative inefficiency can destroy the benefits of other forms of customer service.

Don't blame the service engineer

'I don't believe it. They've given me the wrong part. Those people in the warehouse, they do this every time.'

Does this sound like a familiar problem? The service engineer arrives on site within a guaranteed call-out time and promptly leaves, unable to carry out the repair. The result – an angry customer and a frustrated service engineer who portrays his organisation as inefficient and incompetent. Hardly the recipe for effective customer service, but the situation can be avoided.

Right first time

Here are some tips for ensuring that the service company gets it right first time.

- Whenever you receive a service call, try to assess the parts that are needed.
- If it is difficult to identify the parts, advise the customer and the engineer that a preliminary site visit will be needed to assess requirements.
- Where practical, use pre-packed 'service kits' to ensure that

the right parts are dispatched in line with the engineer's request.

Back up the engineer

If the worst happens and the engineer still finds that the right parts have not been delivered, it is important to limit the damage and reassure the customer that the problem will be resolved quickly and efficiently.

- Provide a dedicated hotline to enable the service engineer to re-order the right parts on emergency delivery.

- Contact the customer and the engineer to advise delivery time and arrange an appointment for the engineer to call.

- Call the customer after the return visit to check that they are completely satisfied with the repair.

- Log any parts problems, monitor performance and introduce corrective actions to improve any bottlenecks or recurring problems.

Motivate support staff

Back-up like this will help to reassure both the engineer and the customer that support staff really are committed to customer satisfaction. It is vital that support staff understand that the quality of service ultimately depends on them. Staff who just pick parts from the shelf probably don't realise how important their role is.

- Tell them about the problems on the customer site.

- Develop a bonus scheme related to quality performance.

- Involve them in improvement programmes.

Build team spirit

The quote at the beginning of this chapter illustrates the reaction that can take place when a service engineer feels let down

174

by colleagues. This frustration can come across to the customer, and that does little to build confidence in the supplier. The engineer probably spends more time in direct contact with the customer than staff who specialise in 'managing' customer relations.

Improving delivery performance

Delivery performance can be a crucial factor in building overall customer satisfaction, but how many organisations see delivery as an area for customer service attention? Here is a set of customer service standards for delivery set by a leading UK manufacturer.

175

Ordering
- We will answer your calls promptly.
- When you place your order, we will agree a delivery date with you and give you an order reference number.

After ordering
- If we are unable to meet a particular timing request, we will inform you the working day before delivery.
- We can provide you with estimated times of arrival (ETA) from 3.30 pm on the working day before delivery.
- Where we have given you an ETA, we will inform you of any subsequent delays immediately.
- If you have any queries or complaints about delivery, we will respond within two working days.

Delivery
- We will deliver to the specified location on the agreed date within the specified operating hours.
- Any change to the agreed delivery date, due to exceptional circumstances, will be carried out in consultation with you.
- If we need to deliver less than the agreed quantity for operational reasons, we will consult you before making any cut to an individual delivery of 10 per cent or more.
- We will observe any pre-agreed delivery instructions.
- All delivery paperwork will be clear and accurate.

These delivery standards help drivers, distribution managers, administrative staff and customers in areas that are often overlooked in customer service programmes. If your company operates its own distribution fleet, assess your operations to see whether they could meet those standards. If you use contract distribution services, ask your contractor for a copy of their standards to see whether they measure up.

Identifying the key areas

The two examples demonstrate the importance of focusing resources and quality processes on mundane activities that can influence customer satisfaction. This approach is applicable to any business where staff actions impinge on customer service. It is particularly appropriate for staff who are not directly in touch with customers and who may be overlooked in a customer care training programme.

In a manufacturing company this might include accounts clerks who produce inaccurate invoices, warehouse staff who pick the wrong parts, or departmental managers who refuse to co-operate in allocating resources to customer-facing activities.

In a service business, it is the people who deliver the service – the technicians and engineers – who are crucial. In some service businesses, they are dealing directly with customers – engineers on site – but in the car business, for example, they are 'hidden away', never exposed to a customer. Any customer complaints are filtered through a series of receptionists and supervisors, and the customer never gets an opportunity to talk directly with the service technician.

Enlightened dealers who recognise the problem have brought service technicians 'out to the front' to talk to customers or have provided customers with viewing areas where they can watch their cars being serviced. Dealers who expose their service staff in this way and made them accountable report that the exercise has a high motivational benefit.

The same process can be applied to professional services where there is a traditional layer of account management between the customer and the service provider. In advertising, for example, the account director, followed by the account manager and an account executive, with perhaps a client services director as well, all stand between the customer and the creative team who develop the advertisements. The creative process also filters down from a creative group head through a creative director to a writer and art director, so the opportunities for low customer awareness are high.

When customer service programmes are valuable

It is the barriers between the customer and the people who provide the service that make customer service programmes so important. These are some business scenarios that indicate when a programme is necessary.

177

- There are high levels of customer complaint with standards of service.

- The complaints can be attributed to poor performance by staff who are not in direct contact with customers, although some of them may be.

- The problems cannot be overcome by quality actions or by change to the physical processes.

- The problems are rooted in poor customer attitudes or a lack of understanding of customer needs.

- There is no mechanism for the key staff to learn about customer needs; the staff are trained in technical skills, but they have no experience of customer care.

- Customer concerns can be identified through surveys and questionnaires, and it is possible to get specific comments from customers.

- Training and other customer actions can be used to improve performance and raise levels of customer satisfaction.

These business scenarios can be applied to a wide range of businesses and help to identify where the customer focus should be placed.

Identifying the problem

- *Can you identify opportunities to raise customer awareness among all levels of staff?*

- *Is lack of customer awareness pulling down customer standards?*

178

- *What are the critical activities that impinge on customer satisfaction?*

- *Can you encourage your customers to put their concerns in writing, and can you promise them a positive response?*

- *What other mechanisms can you use to obtain customer feedback?*

- *Can you utilise existing training programmes to improve performance?*

- *How can you measure and compare performance between different groups?*

A programme to improve performance of all staff

The Ford Motor Company's 'Put Yourself in their Shoes' initiative was a wide-ranging programme that covered all aspects of Ford dealer operations. Ford's overall aim was to improve the quality of service available through dealerships as a means of building long-term customer satisfaction. The objectives of an initiative like 'Put Yourself in their Shoes' include:

- *to raise overall levels of customer satisfaction.*

- *to ensure that individual outlets are able to deliver a consistent standard of service.*

- *to raise awareness of the importance of customer care among staff at all levels.*

- *to make staff aware of customer needs.*

- *to ensure that customer focus is built into all training activities and business processes.*

- *to ensure that customer care activities could be measured.*

Programme operation

The programme began with a process of research using customer complaints and customer feedback as a means of identifying the main causes of concern. The complaints were addressed to both individual dealers and communicated to Ford. The complaints were analysed by Ford and formed patterns so that the company could identify where the main problems were originating. The problems were segmented into the following areas:

- parts department;

- service department;

- bodyshop;

- pre-delivery inspection department.

The programme also identified that the following people would be involved in the process:

- parts manager;

- parts supervisor;

- parts counter staff;

- service manager;

- service receptionist;

- service supervisor;

- service technician.

It was important that senior management in the dealerships were aware of the process of customer focus and were committed to its success, because they would have to allocate time and resources to implement the improvement programme. The medium for getting the information to target staff was brochures and videos, with training guides to support the material.

The programme was initially launched to the dealer body through a series of regional business meetings followed by sales visits to individual dealerships. At the regional business meetings, dealer principals – the senior management team – were given a background briefing on the importance of the programme and given individual launch packs that explained how the programmes were to be operated.

The company also introduced a series of complementary initiatives to add a competitive element to the programme. Dealership staff who reached the required standard in their own activities were invited to join specialist staff guilds and compete against each other to be 'Service Receptionist of the Year' or 'Technician of the Year'. This inter-dealer rivalry was important to the long-term success of the programme because it paved the way for the introduction of nationwide customer focus standards in the future. The regional business meetings helped to build commitment to the programme at senior level and paved the way for the individual dealer launch.

The programme was too important just to send a brochure and video to dealers and let them get on with it. Sales staff who were responsible for dealer liaison and development visited each dealer to hold an introductory session and to discuss an implementation plan with each dealership. The programme was introduced to key members of staff who had been identified earlier in the programme.

A video which explained the overall aims of the programme was used to introduce the sessions, and the Ford representative then worked with individual groups to help them identify ways in which they could improve their performance. The basis of the improvement programmes was a selection of customer comments which covered common faults with the product or the service: 'the ashtray was full and I'm a non-smoker', 'they left grease all over the steering wheel', 'I found the same fault even though I had described it in detail to the service receptionist'.

Benefits of the programme

181

The programme enabled Ford to build a commitment to customer care among staff who felt that they had little to do with customers, and laid the groundwork for future customer care programmes that were targeted at different groups of staff. By using customer comments directly, they helped staff to look at their work from the customer's point of view and to treat each customer as an individual.

The programme also encouraged an attitude of competition between different groups of staff and this allowed progress to be measured. Comparing the customer care rating of different departments or different dealerships allows Ford to take action to improve under-performing dealerships and to reward achievement.

Customers benefit because they receive higher standards of service and they can be confident that their concerns will be recognised. By telling the company about their problems, they are encouraging and receiving a positive response. They can expect that their cars will be taken care of and returned in the best possible condition.

Putting the programme into operation

These are the key stages in putting a programme like this into operation:

- *Identify the people who are the target for the programme.*

- *Use customer research to assess the planned outcome of the programme.*

- *Develop a training programme that will improve staff performance.*

- *Encourage staff to develop their own action programmes.*

- *Measure and reward improvements in performance.*

- *Provide a basis for comparison between different groups of staff.*

- *Get the commitment of managers to support the programme by demonstrating business benefits.*

- *Provide support and resources to implement the programme at local level.*

- *Ensure that customer queries and concerns receive a positive response.*

- *Involve customers in the process of improving standards and keep them informed of progress.*

Summary

The less glamorous company activities, such as administration, distribution or maintenance can have a significant impact on customer satisfaction, so it is important to help people understand customers by directly relaying customer comments to 'backroom staff'. The customer comments represent common problems in customer relations and encourage the staff to recognise their customers' concerns and take action. Action programmes should be put into place to improve performance, and there should be a basis for measuring progress and comparative performance.

Measure customer service performance

Introduction

When you set customer service standards, how can you be sure that your staff are maintaining those standards? Measurement has traditionally been applied to mechanical processes or financial performance, but the use of quality processes can ensure that you are delivering the right level of customer service consistently.

A local council sets out standards for the way it handles enquiries. It promises amongst other things to:

- respond to incoming telephone calls within three rings; that applies to calls within departments, as well as calls reaching the switchboard;
- return all calls that failed to reach the original point of contact within an hour;
- reply to all written enquiries within three days of receipt;
- carry out a range of activities such as searches or requests for information within agreed time limits.

Quality is increasingly used as a means of measuring standards of customer service. Quality standards can be applied and adapted to different types of business. Quality standards must be measurable; they should be carefully controlled and, ideally, they should conform to the standards of an independent organisation such as the British Standards Institute (BSI). The British Standards Institute manages a broad range of standards for products and services. Product standards, for example, mean that products have been manufactured and inspected to extremely tight specifications, and customers can feel confident that any batch of products coming from one company or from a number of sources will be consistent in quality.

The importance of service measurement

Service measurement and feedback are important in a number of scenarios:

- when a company is operating through a number of different outlets and wants to offer consistent standards through every outlet;
- when services are critical to a customer's business success and quality measurement provides a competitive advantage;
- when a company wants to demonstrate high levels of customer care.

Measuring the quality of service

Quality techniques are now being applied to the standards of service available from a company, and BS 5750 is the recognised means of demonstrating that a business conforms to international quality standards in the way it deals with customers. Not a set of rigid standards applied in the same way to every business, BS 5750 measures the business in a number of different fields that are crucial to the quality of customer service. So BS 5750 would be applied in different ways to a manufacturing company and to a professional services consultancy. Each company is measured and can be compared easily and realistically.

Service performance can therefore be included in the scope of BS 5750. A group of solicitors, for example, decided that it would be worth registering under BS 5750 to demonstrate that they were capable of delivering a quality professional service. The initial assessment was used to identify the critical activities which determined the successful operation of the practice. The assessment covered general activities such as speed of response to telephone and written enquiries, and more specific activities such as time spent in handling conveyancing or searches. Consultants worked with the practice management team to define a unique set of standards and to identify the actions that would be needed to achieve that standard in each of the branches.

The consultants drew up a timetable for achieving the standards and, when the practice had achieved them, it was awarded BS 5750. The process did not stop there, because each branch had to continue to meet the performance standards to retain its status as a BS 5750 supplier. The practice was able to control the performance of each of its branches and was able to offer its clients a measurable standard of service.

187

Measuring customer response times

A company that had a number of local branches set up a central point of contact for customer enquiries throughout the country. Customer response was previously handled by individual branches dealing with their local customers, but branches did not necessarily have the skills or resources needed to deal with the full range of enquiries. The key processes of the customer reception centre conform to BS 5750, and this helps to provide customers with a quality response to all their queries.

Customer reception staff are measured on how quickly they reply to the original call, how quickly they provide a response within specific guidelines and how frequently they keep the customer informed until the task is completed. There is also an integral escalation procedure so that any queries that cannot be handled within target times are immediately handed on to other people within the organisation who have the authority to commit additional resources to the problem.

Measuring the consistency of service

Local service stations are now starting to use BS 5750; a number of car dealerships, for example, now have service departments which conform to BS 5750, and this provides service customers with a reassurance of quality. Service technicians have always followed the guidelines of manufacturer's approved service schedules, but the new requirements of BS 5750 have added additional inspection processes and different work practices which improve the quality of the service department.

For example, incomplete jobs which might be waiting for replacement parts are labelled 'process incomplete', so that the vehicle is not accidentally moved while it is in a possibly dangerous condition. Other aspects of BS 5750 relate to the time taken to complete jobs, presentation and explanation of invoices and procedures for dealing with customer complaints. This improved quality of service and the seal of approval of an independent organisation helped to enhance the reputation of an area of the motor trade that has traditionally suffered from a poor reputation and it also enables the manufacturer to offer customers a consistent standard of service throughout the branch network.

188

Measuring customers' expectations of quality

Registration with the BSI provides an independent method of assessing and maintaining the quality of branch performance. Quality can also be assessed in line with customers' expectations of the service. Research into customers' attitudes shows how customers feel about the service that is being delivered.

For example, many service organisations provide a questionnaire to customers at the end of every service asking how they rated different aspects of the service. The service engineers are also asked to complete a visit report describing the nature of the problem, the actions they took and the time taken to complete different aspects of the job. By analysing this information and comparing the performance of individual branches and individual engineers, the company can build up a profile of service performance and can take appropriate action to deal with any of the problems.

The performance survey covers such aspects as:

- time to reach customer;
- promptness of arrival;
- time to diagnose;
- availability of replacement parts;
- time to complete the task;
- satisfaction with the standard of work;
- helpfulness of the service engineer.

189

The fact that part of the measurement is based on actual customer assessment rather than a set of arbitrary standards gives greater credibility to the results, and enables them to be presented as part of a customer focus programme. The customer surveys also provide an opportunity to maintain proactive communication with customers by showing that local outlets respond to customer queries and concerns.

Measuring performance in quality is however only the starting point for achieving consistency. The customer surveys and the quality assessment indicate the key factors to be measured and the level of current achievement. The challenge to the supplier is how to raise and maintain the quality of performance throughout the local network.

Measuring feedback

It is important that you obtain regular feedback from your customers to ensure that they are achieving the right level of customer satisfaction. Consultation on new product developments or participation in liaison committees and user groups allow you to take account of your customers' views, while effective complaints procedures demonstrate that you can deal with problems and respond effectively. There are many other ways of obtaining feedback, using techniques such as:

- **customer satisfaction surveys;**
- **service cards;**
- **telephone surveys;**
- **review meetings.**

Benefits of the programme

By utilising quality-driven measurements, a company can impose consistent performance standards on different groups and outlets. Quality standards provide an independent form of measurement that ensures a valid means of comparison. By utilising customer feedback mechanisms, it is possible to focus improvement on customers' needs.

190

What to measure

What are the critical customer-facing activities and how can they be measured?

- *Can independent quality standards be used to measure performance?*
- *Can you use customer feedback techniques such as service questionnaires or telephone follow up to measure customer attitudes?*
- *Do you build improvement mechanisms into your measurement programmes?*

Paying the price for customer service

A high street bank told its customers that it will pay them if it makes a mistake. The bank has published a charter which sets out its standards for service. The charter covers the following points:

- It will not make errors on statements.
- It will set up and pay standing orders without mistakes.
- It will automatically issue cheque books and cards to ensure that customers always have them when they need them.
- They will give decisions on overdrafts and personal loans immediately, and have funds available within an hour of agreement.
- They will open new accounts within 48 hours of application.

191

If the bank makes a mistake on any of those points, the customer will receive £10.

A leading health insurance company offers an equally flexible approach. They promise their corporate customers that if they fail to meet standards or miss deadlines, they will pay compensation. For example, for a delay in issuing settlement cheques, the company pays £5, but if it fails to notify customers of renewal dates three weeks in advance, they pay £100.

The company reports that its corporate clients are not specifically interested in the money itself, but they appreciate that the gesture demonstrates the company's commitment to quality customer service. Demonstrating commitment in this way shows customers that you are serious about your standards. These are some of the actions you can take to implement a customer service payment system in your organisation:

- *Identify the factors that customers feel most strongly about.*
- *Set customer performance standards for each factor.*

- *Introduce training programmes to ensure high levels of performance.*
- *Tell customers about the standards and explain the methods of compensation.*
- *Measure performance.*

Summary

Quality techniques can be applied to the measurement and control of customer service as a means of monitoring performance and improving standards. Quality standards provide a valuable competitive differentiator and demonstrate a commitment to customer service. It is important to apply quality standards to customer-facing tasks, and to involve customers in assessing performance. You can show customers that you are really committed to your standards by offering them compensation if you fail to meet the measures you have imposed.

24

Monitor customer satisfaction levels

Introduction

Satisfied customers mean repeat business and high levels of customer loyalty. To ensure that you are delivering the highest standards of customer satisfaction, you need to continuously measure satisfaction levels and ensure that your findings are used to improve performance.

Focusing people on customer satisfaction

The most important aspect of any programme is to focus people on customer satisfaction and this can be achieved in a number of ways:

- issuing customer focus standards to ensure consistent standards;
- introducing customer care programmes which give a high profile to the whole process of customer care;
- introducing customer satisfaction ratings to measure how well the company is performing;
- operating customer satisfaction incentive schemes to reward people who have achieved the highest levels of customer satisfaction.

Using customer focus standards to improve satisfaction

Customer focus standards determine how well the business is run in the eyes of customers. Many franchised and independent distributors have to conform to operating requirements as part of their distributor agreement. Typically, these would cover the size of the premises, facilities, stock levels, head count, capital funding, management skills and training requirements to ensure that the branch was able to provide the level of service covered by their agreement.

An increasing number of companies are introducing customer focus standards as part of their agreement to improve levels of customer satisfaction. The Post Office, for example, is moving many of its main post offices from central high street positions to new locations within large retail outlets or to out-of-town shopping centres. Part of the reason for the change is to reduce the cost of maintaining an expensive town centre position, but they are also taking the opportunity to move to premises that are more convenient for their customers and to improve the quality of service.

Many were relocated within retail outlets and were able to offer longer opening hours, plus the convenience of offering their customers the chance to do other shopping at the same time. The out-of-town locations offered even greater convenience with adequate parking, wheelchair access, spacious premises and the same opportunities for longer opening hours and one-stop shopping. These retailing developments, together with future developments in counter automation, training and an increasing range of products and services were at the heart of the Post Office's drive to become a more customer-focused organisation serving the needs of the local market.

A number of American-style pizza home delivery services are run as franchise operations, and they aim to improve the quality and consistency of their service by introducing customer focus standards. They realise that, in a fiercely competitive market,

194

they have to establish a strong brand identity, and that identity is based not just on the quality of the pizza but on the quality of service. Many of the operators offer a guaranteed home delivery time backed by a full refund if they fail to meet the time.

They want to attract customers by offering the convenience of home delivery, but they have suffered in the past from inconsistent delivery performance, with the pizzas arriving unacceptably late or arriving cold. The promise to deliver on time or provide a refund is a powerful motivator for the local staff since failure hits directly at their profit levels.

Direct Line Insurance has introduced high levels of convenience and rapid response into the car insurance market, and shows that a successful and profitable business can be built on customer focus standards. The company accepts enquiries through a well-trained customer reception centre. The customers are guided through a series of simple questions, and the respondent then provides an immediate quotation. If the customer wishes to proceed, the respondent issues immediate cover without any further administration or form filling. Claims are handled in a similar way.

195

The result for the customer is a service that is simple, responsive, convenient and good value for money. Direct Line have the advantage that they handle incoming enquiries centrally, but other organisations can use the same principles to establish a customer-focused service.

Improving satisfaction through customer care programmes

Customer care programmes provide companies with the means to improve customer care performance. For example, most car manufacturers now offer a courtesy vehicle service to their service customers. Research identified that convenience was the biggest factor in selecting a service outlet. Many motorists felt that they could not do without some form of transport. Service centres which were located near homes, places of work or public transport routes were appealing to customers – and car dealers which could not offer similar levels of convenience were losing business. Some car dealers offered their customers lower-price car rental when their vehicles were in for repair, but this still represented an additional cost and was a poor alternative.

Manufacturers introduced the concept of courtesy vehicles and set up fleets at dealerships around the country. The service was optional and dealers were encouraged to offer the vehicles to customers who were likely to suffer the most inconvenience as a result of their cars being off the road. The programme operating guide identified these as business users, doctors, nurses, mothers with young children and others. The intention was to emphasise that the courtesy vehicle was a discretionary offer and not an automatic offer with every service. The customer was to recognise that the dealership was making a genuine attempt to reduce inconvenience and offer greater standards of customer care.

Home builders, recognising that customers may have concerns about the quality of their new homes, have introduced customer care visits at set periods after the customers have moved in. The customer care visits gave customers the opportunity to discuss any queries or problems they might have about their new homes. The programme allows the company to take the initiative and defuse any potentially damaging complaints. This works only if the homebuilders implement a quality building programme and are prepared to carry out remedial work to high quality standards.

Putting right defective work is not in itself a customer care programme, but taking positive steps to offer a proactive response is. If the programme succeeds, customers will perceive that the homebuilder is a caring company and is prepared to respond to customer needs. This is an important form of local marketing support because it brands the homebuilder and, when customers move, they will be encouraged to buy another house from the same builder.

Given that householders may move on average every five years, the customer care programme is an important factor in customer loyalty.

Building satisfaction through customer care training

The second part of the customer care equation is attitude – ensuring that staff are committed to the highest standards of customer care. The customer care training industry is now highly developed and there are a wide variety of general-purpose and tailored training programmes available.

Videos, such as the Video Arts series on caring for the customer, have established an excellent reputation. *The Sunday Times* publishes videos and books on customer care, and there are numerous conferences and training organisations offering individual programmes. The problem is not in obtaining training material, but knowing how to apply it.

197

Ford have renamed their Technical Training Centre the Ford Care Institute because this reflects the central role that customer care plays at every level in the industry. Technicians who serviced cars were not traditionally regarded as contributors to customer care, but if they did a poor job this reflected on customer satisfaction. Included in the technical training programmes were modules on cleanliness of the vehicle, checking workmanship, using protective covers to prevent grease marks, and tips on returning the vehicle in the condition it arrived, with seats and mirrors in the same position, radio tuned to the correct frequency, ashtrays emptied and most important, the car working properly.

An increasing number of companies recognise the contribution that good administration makes to effective customer relations and they are training their staff in the virtues of accurate invoicing. Accurate invoicing obviously helps the company's own cashflow by reducing the number of errors and speeding up payment, but it also helps to reduce the customers' administration burden of checking and querying invoices. A supplier can provide material and personal support to local outlets to ensure that the same standards are maintained. It can issue material support in the form of standard accounting packages and procedures and it can provide training in the importance and techniques of accurate invoicing.

It's just as important to train the managers and supervisors of staff responsible for customer care so that they are prepared to commit time and resources to training. When British Airways launched their long-term programme to improve the quality of customer service before privatisation, they introduced a comprehensive management training programme before they began training the people who delivered the customer service in the front line. It was essential, they believed, that managers should understand the problems customer service staff faced and provide them with the proper levels of support.

Customer satisfaction ratings

Customer care is a business discipline that can be managed and measured. It ensures that the company can retain customers and ensure future income and profitability. In terms of customer care performance, the customer satisfaction index is the most efficient method of measuring achievement and improvement.

Customer satisfaction index

A customer satisfaction index takes the results from a number of satisfaction surveys and allocates a numerical value to key customer satisfaction indicators. A department or company is then given an overall index of performance which can be compared with other groups and measured on a year-on-year basis. Customer satisfaction ratings are a direct method of assessing customer care performance and they provide a means for motivating people to improved customer care standards.

Customer satisfaction surveys

The basis of customer satisfaction ratings is a customer satisfaction survey. This is sent to customers who have purchased a product or service at intervals, a week or a month after purchase, for example, and six months or a year after initial purchase.

The first questionnaire is to establish the customers' response to the way the sale was handled, and the second to establish how the customer feels about the product or service in use and how they feel about the aftercare they have received from the outlet. The questionnaire asks customers to respond to questions with a scale of satisfaction – fully satisfied, very satisfied, satisfied, not very satisfied, very dissatisfied – or alternatively asked to respond on a numerical scale, 'on a scale of 1–10, how satisfied were you with . . . . 1 is very dissatisfied, 10 is very satisfied'. Customers can also provide written comments on aspects of the service and, in some cases, ask for specific actions such as an explanation from the departmental manager.

A first-stage questionnaire might include such questions as,

How satisfied are you with:
- the response of sales staff;
- the location and convenience of the staff;
- convenience of opening hours;
- ease of parking;
- availability of product information;
- product knowledge of staff;
- waiting time to be served;
- choice of payment methods;
- explanation of options;
- presentation of product;
- availability of finance;
- explanation of aftercare?

The questionnaire which followed up at six months or a year after purchase would focus on customer satisfaction with the product or service and the quality of aftercare. It might include questions such as,

How satisfied are you with:

- the quality and performance of the product;
- the reliability of the product;
- the benefits of the service;
- the standard of the service;
- the response of the branch to any queries;
- the value of any instruction manuals;
- the quality of aftercare service;
- the standard and speed of aftercare;
- the value of the warranty;
- availability of replacement parts;
- flexibility of service plans;
- availability of accessories?

The two types of questionnaire are designed to assess how much effort the outlet is putting into selling the product properly; i.e., does the customer believe the outlet is trying to help him select the right product? The answers to the questions can be used to assess the performance of the salesforce and the quality of product information. The questions on convenience can also act as a guide to the convenience of the store and help to plan changes or improvements.

The second questionnaire seeks to find out how well the outlet is faring during the critical period after the sale. It reminds the customer that there is life after the sale, and helps to build contact during the critical period between sales when the customer could easily be influenced by offers from another manufacturer. If the customer is satisfied with all aspects of the outlet's service – product, convenience, quality and aftercare – it is likely that the customer will return to that outlet for his next purchase.

Responding to surveys

If they do not indicate satisfaction, the outlet has an opportunity to take remedial action or to respond to the customer's concerns. The real importance of a customer satisfaction index is whether it generates action and improves business performance. The index must be carefully weighted to focus the attention of the local outlet on the key indicators of customer satisfaction. Each response is given a score and the totals of all customer responses are added up to give an overall index for the outlet. The index may be based on the answers to all questions, or it may be based on a selection of questions which are most important to overall satisfaction.

Car dealerships, for example, concentrate on the response to aftercare – 'how satisfied were you with the service from the parts and service departments' – because they know that the key to retaining customers between new car sales is the two- to three-year period when the customer deals with the parts and service departments. One European manufacturer calculated that the new car sales process generated a possible 1 million contacts per year, while aftercare generated a potential 5 million contacts. It was vital that their aftercare programmes were perceived well by the customer.

201

This pattern will vary by type of purchase.

- In fast-moving consumer goods, for example, purchasing frequency is much higher; aftercare would play a minor role in customer satisfaction, while convenience, quality of checkout service, price, choice, parking, and opening hours would be more crucial.
- In the marketing of complex business-to-business products and services, the quality of advice and guidance, the level of pre-sales and aftersales support, and the contribution of other key long-term customer services are crucial factors which determine how well customers may benefit.

Customer satisfaction guides

The customer satisfaction index, by itself, has little value. It gives an indication of how customers rate performance, and provides a method of comparison, but unless people take action to build on their strengths or improve their weaknesses, the questionnaire will be wasted. When a department is participating in a customer satisfaction programme, they should be given a programme guide outlining the reasons for the programme, the business benefits, and the actions the department must take as a result of the programme.

Scope of the guide

Ford's customer satisfaction programme guide is a comprehensive publication aimed at the dealer principal and the dealership management team. It covers:

- the importance of customer satisfaction;
- the scope of the programme;
- the survey which is the basis of the programme;
- the reasons for the questions;
- the method of calculating the index;
- the management actions that should be taken in response to the questionnaire;
- a department by department guide to key customer concerns that have already been identified;
- a summary of actions that other dealers have taken to meet those concerns;
- a development programme for the dealership;
- the training and business programmes available to improve customer satisfaction performance.

Action plans

The most important sections are the management actions and the departmental guides. A customer satisfaction index is simply a starting point for building a business that is focused on the customer. The programme manual recommends a series of meetings:

- **a fortnightly review** of all the responses received from customers during the previous period – all questionnaires are returned to a handling agency who analyses the responses, and forwards results and requests for action to individual dealerships once a fortnight;

- **a monthly review** of action taken in response to the questionnaire;
- **a quarterly review** of improvements in individual areas and in overall customer satisfaction.

At the fortnightly meetings, departmental managers are given the results of the previous questionnaire and asked to respond to any immediate requests from customers or to deal with any serious complaints within the questionnaires. If, for example, a customer says that they are extremely dissatisfied with a 36,000 mile service, the service manager will be told to contact the customer immediately to find out more information and make an immediate response.

The monthly meetings should focus on more general concerns. If, for example, a large number of customers say they are dissatisfied with parking arrangements or length of time spent in customer reception, the dealership can take action to improve the situation.

203

The quarterly meeting is a more formal review of progress in improvements and trends in customer satisfaction performance. The dealer principal should take the opportunity to review current improvement projects and to assess whether earlier improvement programmes have had a direct effect on overall customer satisfaction performance levels.

Outlining departmental responsibility

The departmental guides within the customer satisfaction manual are intended to give individual departments a clearer indication of their contribution to customer satisfaction and outline the actions they can take to improve performance. In a questionnaire on standards of service, for example, customers commented on grease marks on their car, cigarettes in the ashtray, radios tuned to a different frequency, or a fault recurring despite the service.

These comments, taken from actual questionnaires, demonstrated to members of staff who don't normally meet customers that there are good reasons for concentrating on customer care, and they show that the department's contribution is important. The section also includes practical examples of what other dealers have done to improve performance in this area. This helps dealers to put together their own action plans.

The customer satisfaction performance guide can be a valuable method of implementing customer care programmes within an outlet, but it must be an action-oriented programme which local managers can put to immediate use.

Summary

This section shows why high standards of customer care are essential to building customer satisfaction and loyalty. It also show the importance of measuring customer satisfaction through customer surveys and how customer comments can be used to compile customer satisfaction guides.

Reward customer service excellence

Customer satisfaction incentive schemes

The customer satisfaction index described in the previous chapter can be used to encourage improvement using recognition and incentive programmes. By providing a quantitative basis for comparison, departments and individuals can compete with each other to demonstrate that they offer the highest levels of satisfaction. This competitive element can be used in a number of ways:

- *to incentivise individuals and groups to improve their own performance on a year-on-year basis;*
- *to incentivise individuals to improve their own performance;*
- *to encourage the highest standards of customer satisfaction.*

The incentive programmes should be based, not just on current performance, but on improvement and it must continue to recognise improvement over a long period of time. Most programmes however recognise improvement and they can be based on departmental or regional groupings.

Top-performing groups in a league receive an award or a prize. A higher status of award can be given to the outlets who achieve the very highest levels of customer satisfaction. A number of programmes operating under the banner of chairman's or president's award recognise excellence in customer satisfaction with a special award for an élite group of branches. Ford's Chairman's Award is an élite pan-European award given to the top dealers in each of 16 territories; they are taken to a top European destination where they are personally recognised by the chairman of Ford of Europe.

Programmes like this help to maintain the impetus of customer care programmes; they ensure that individuals, departments and branches aim at continually improving standards.

Why rewards and recognition are important

Service providers rarely receive feedback from customers explaining how pleased they are with the service provided. Unlike sales people, they are not in a position to receive the sort of instant recognition and boost of self-esteem that comes with making a sale.

It is important to make sure that customer service staff are being recognised and rewarded for good service in all areas, at all levels and in all jobs. People who understand that they will be rewarded for achievements are instantly motivated to improve. Management should realise that providing rewards and recognition is a well established form of developing motivation on the job, and it can dramatically improve an organisation's customer service.

Make the goal clear to people, explain how incentives will help to build a totally customer-focused organisation. It is possible that as an organisation becomes more and more customer focused, there are individuals who are simply not capable of providing the levels of service customers are demanding.

Elements of an effective reward system

- **Set clear targets.**
- **Provide flexible rewards.**
- **Deliver the reward quickly with impact.**

- **Provide the reward personally.**
- **Reward what truly matters.**

Set clear targets

It's vital that everyone knows what is being measured and how it is being measured. If the programme rewards departmental achievement, how will it be measured? Will it be using a method based on the customer's point of view, i.e., on the results of a customer satisfaction survey, or on some more concrete measure such as percentage of telephone calls answered within the target time? There must be a way to measure which service providers are more successful than others. It is important that the service provider is involved in developing the targets and agrees that they are realistic and objective.

Provide flexible rewards

207

The reward scheme should appeal to everyone in the programme. For example, a gift catalogue which offered winners a wide choice of quality products offers flexibility, but a weekend's horeseriding may not have universal appeal. Gift vouchers are perhaps the most flexible type of reward, allowing winners to choose their own rewards, although they lack the immediacy of a product.

It can be difficult to develop an award programme that meets all requirements. A company might argue that all of its service providers are excellent top performers. It is impossible to distinguish one as being better than the others. A flexible award programme can overcome this problem.

Deliver the reward quickly with impact

Annual awards may be suitable for high-achieving customer service performers, but if the objective is to achieve a large number of small improvements in service, it may be better to operate more regular awards. A lot of companies hold weekly or monthly 'rallies' where top achievers are acknowledged and rewarded. This provides a degree of immediacy and also encourages people to focus on specific target. Short-term awards can also operate in tandem with longer-term programmes that reward consistent high performers.

Provide the reward personally

The 'rallies' described in the previous section enable the company to recognise high achievers in the presence of their colleagues. Ideally the awards should be presented by a senior member of staff or by someone who is recognised as a customer service achiever.

However, public performances may not always be appropriate. Choose the method which is most comfortable for the service provider receiving the reward. In some instances service providers would prefer private recognition rather than a public display.

Reward what is important

It is important that the award programmes are focused on the most important customer satisfaction tasks. When you carry out customer satisfaction surveys, identify the factors that customers feel are most important and use these as the basis of award programmes. Because every organisation has its own individual style, approach and culture there are no set rules. The key elements of an effective reward system are only guidelines which must be interpreted with flexibility.

Celebrate minor successes

Customer service managers are able to directly influence the performance of service providers by looking for opportunities to recognise small achievements. This approach is in addition to any reward or recognition systems and programmes developed to build motivation. Service providers generally don't or rarely receive a direct pat on the back from their manager for the extra effort they put in for customers. Celebrating the tiny successes along the way is a necessity. Although it is impossible for a customer service manager to celebrate all of the successes day in and day out, they can encourage an environment where service providers celebrate their own successes.

Provide positive feedback

When providing feedback to service providers, first focus attention on the specific action or accomplishment and provide the individual with recognition.

Platitudes and generalisations are not motivating feedback in any sense. Vague compliments after a period of time promote a demotivating rather than motivating environment due to their perceived insincerity. Always be specific with compliments and feedback.

Summary

Customer service award schemes play an important part in achieving and maintaining high levels of customer satisfaction. Award programmes allow the performance of individuals and departments to be compared and evaluated over a period of time. It is important to develop a flexible approach to award programmes – they must be suitable for the participants and for the overall programme goals. The intention is to motivate people to improve their performance at every level and not just to achieve.

Index

■